4$ 14.95

THE ANATOMY
OF JUDGEMENT

D0796991

UNIVERSITY LIBRARY
LOMA LINDA, CALIFORNIA

THE ANATOMY
OF JUDGEMENT

AN INVESTIGATION INTO THE PROCESSES
OF PERCEPTION AND REASONING

M. L. Johnson Abercrombie

'*an association in which the free development of each*
is the condition of the free development of all'

Free Association Books / London / 1989

UNIVERSITY LIBRARY

Published in Great Britain in 1989 by
Free Association Books
26 Freegrove Road
London N7 9RQ

First published 1960

Copyright © M. L. Johnson Abercrombie 1960

British Library Cataloguing in Publication Data
Abercrombie, M. L. J. (Minnie Louise Johnson), 1909–1984
The anatomy of judgement.
1. Judgement
I. Title
153.4'6

ISBN 1-85343-106-0

Printed and bound in Great Britain by
Bookcraft, Midsomer Norton, Avon

Contents

List of Plates

Line Diagrams

Publisher's Foreword

Because it is so lucid and clear, this book needs little introduction except for the purpose of emphasizing its current relevance. It is an utterly accessible, empirically-based introduction to the unconscious dimensions of perception and judgement. In particular, the author shows with great eloquence just how complicated and subject to context are the supposedly most unequivocal facts – those of science.

The relevance to the present is that there is an important coming together of ideas from psychoanalysis and philosophy, so that a psychoanalytic theory of knowledge is in sight, though not yet in sharp focus. We have in the work of M. L. Johnson Abercrombie a synthesis of ideas and research from group analysis, the psychology of perception and the philosophy of science. Abercrombie applies them to the learning process of applied scientists, namely medical students. Using group analytic methods derived from S. H. Foulkes, she then shows how group explorations can shed light on the processes by which we come to have experiences which we believe to be unequivocal.

I suggest that this book is an essential introduction to a psychoanalytic epistemology of everyday life and of science. I read it when it was first published in 1960; its insights have remained with me, and its relevance to the present strikes me as considerable.

Robert M. Young
Spring 1989

Acknowledgments

I am indebted to M. Abercrombie, B. C. Brookes, H. F. Brookes, Jean MacGibbon, L. E. R. Picken, and J. Z. Young for criticizing one or other drafts of this book, and to Maureen T. Blazey and Pauline Gregory for invaluable secretarial assistance. Many flaws have been removed as a result of their labour and their interest has sustained me.

For making possible the work that this book reports, I am deeply grateful to Professor J. Z. Young, to the Rockefeller Foundation, and to preclinical students at University College, London, in whose company I spent many delightful and profitable hours.

The work was strongly influenced by that of S. H. Foulkes on group analytic psychotherapy, and by that of the late Adelbert Ames, Jr., and others who have researched on the projective nature of perception. I wish to record my gratitude to them and to the many others who have contributed to the work, knowingly or unknowingly, either by personal contact or by their writings.

Finally, acknowledgements are due to the following for permission to reproduce illustrations. *The American Journal of Psychology* (Fig. 1). American Psychological Assn. (Fig. 6). *Centre d'Etudes et Documentation Préhistoriques* (Plates II A and III A, from *Four Hundred Years of Cave Art*, by H. Breuil). Harper and Brothers (Fig. 8). *Horizons de France* (Plates II B and III B, from *Le Monde des Mammifères*, by F. Bourlière). Dr. F. P. Kilpatrick (Fig. 9 and Plate VI). Kunsthistorisches Museum (Plate I). The Prehistoric Society (Fig. 7). The Readers' Digest Association Ltd. and *This Week* (Fig. 3, from the British Edition, Nov., 1954). *Verlag Hans Huber* (Plate IV, from *Psychodiagnostics*, by H. Rorschach.)

To

MY MOTHER,

MY HUSBAND, &

MY SON

Introduction: The Anatomy of Judgment

On getting information

All day and every day we are receiving information through our sense organs. Some of it is immediately useful and we act on it, as when we stop to avoid crashing into a car, pick up a piece of food to put it in our mouth, or lift the telephone receiver when the bell rings. Much of it is not immediately useful; we are aware of receiving it but we do nothing about it, as when we refrain from answering somebody else's telephone, or take notice that it is raining or fine although we are not going out. Still other information is received without our being immediately conscious of it—as when we can recall something we must have seen, as we say, without noticing it. Whether or not we act on this information and whether or not we are conscious of it, much of it is stored and may affect our subsequent behaviour.

Our efficiency in living our lives as ordinary human beings depends on what we do with this bombardment of information: what we ignore in it, what guidance to immediate action we accept from it, how we store it and how we use the store. Crossing the road safely obviously involves selection; we disregard available information about, say, shop-window displays and pay attention to traffic. But there is more to it than this: we make guesses about the future from things we notice in the present. Our decision when to cross the road, though made apparently in a flash, depends on estimates based on past experience of similar situations; about, for instance, the speed of a car, the skill of a cyclist, the temper of a taxi driver, our own nimbleness, the state of the road surface and the behaviour of other pedestrians; and is perhaps also influenced by an article on road accidents we have recently read. If we have made a good guess we shall have predicted correctly where we shall be in relation to the approaching traffic during all the time taken to make the crossing and we shall get safely over the road.

Thus our reacting to the present bombardment of information involves ignoring some of it, seizing the rest and interpreting it in the light of past experience in order to make as good a guess as possible about what is going to happen. This may be called a process of *judgment*; that is, making a 'decision or conclusion on the basis of indications and probabilities when the facts are not clearly ascertained' (Webster, 1934). We are continually selecting from the information presented, interpreting it with information received in the past, and making predictions about the future.

How distant this future is varies. Sometimes it is the immediate future we are concerned with as in crossing the road, or in choosing an apple to eat. When we choose what we think is the nicest apple from a plateful, we are guessing about how our teeth, tongue and palate will react to it in the next moment as we bite it. But if we are choosing apples to store for the winter we are guessing about what changes will have taken place over the next few months in their texture and taste, their water, sugar and acid content, etc. When we plan a picnic we rely on predictions of the temperature and rainfall over say twelve hours; when we plant potatoes, over several months; when we plant trees, over several years. Whether short term or long, our predictions are based on our own experience of similar events, and on what we have been able to learn from other people's. Science is such experience organized as a body of knowledge, and applied science is concerned with making more reliable our predictions about things of practical importance. The study of astronomy and the development of the calendar for instance were associated with predictions for planting and reaping. As a result of systematizing information, of pooling and organizing many people's experience, we can make new, more general and more accurate predictions and make them about events more distant in place and time, than we can if we use only our own personal experience.

It is with the factors that influence the making of judgments, and particularly judgments in science, that this book is concerned. The material was collected during ten years of research into the problems of teaching students to be 'scientific' or 'objective' or, in more precise terms, to obtain information of good predictive value from a given situation. The research led along diverse paths to fields far away from what is commonly regarded as 'science', and it is necessary to give a brief history of the project in order to explain how matters usually excluded from consideration were found to be relevant to the problems of training scientists.

The teaching project

The history of the project is as follows. As a teacher of zoology I had been disappointed in the effects that learning about science seemed to have on habits of thinking (Bauer and Johnson, 1946; Johnson, 1948). It was found that students who had satisfied the examiners for the Higher School Certificate that they were well grounded in the facts of biology, physics and chemistry, did not necessarily use scientific ways of thinking to solve problems presented in a slightly new way. They might be able, for instance, to recite all the lines of evidence for the theory of evolution but yet be unable to use this material to defend the theory in argument with an anti-evolutionist. They might know what the function of a certain organ is believed to be, but did not always know why, nor did they clearly understand on what kind of evidence a belief of that sort was based. When asked to describe what they saw in dissecting an animal, or in looking through a microscope, they often did not distinguish sufficiently sharply between what was there and what they had been taught 'ought' to be there. The effect on students of two or three years' teaching at the University was no more encouraging. It seemed that scientific ways of thinking did not automatically result from learning the facts of science and that a more radical approach to training was necessary.

After the war there was great interest in the problems of selecting and training medical students, and I was fortunate to have the opportunity of working in this field under Professor J. Z. Young in the Department of Anatomy at University College, London, and with the financial support of the Rockefeller Foundation. A statement in the Report of a Committee of the Royal College of Physicians (1944), one of the bodies that had deliberated on the problems of medical education, served as a text for our guidance. The average medical graduate, the Committee said, 'tends to lack curiosity and initiative; his powers of observation are relatively undeveloped; his ability to arrange and interpret facts is poor; he lacks precision in the use of words.'

By this time, realizing that some of these difficulties of 'being scientific' were related to general attitudes or personal predispositions, I had begun to teach through discussion among small groups of students. This involved, as we shall see in Chapter 5, a different relationship between teacher and student, and between students, than is usual in University teaching. I soon encountered opposition aroused by the unfamiliarity of the situation, ranging from polite expression of disapproval or bewilderment to scarcely veiled, or even open, hostility. By good chance, I commented to a colleague that this behaviour resembled that of patients in group psychotherapy I had seen reported, and through him I was introduced to a psychiatrist who invited me to see a therapeutic group he was then conducting. This was an illuminating experience for me, and I felt that if one could transfer to a teaching group something of the atmosphere he had established in this therapeutic group, new ways of seeing and thinking might be encouraged. I therefore joined a therapeutic group conducted by Dr. S. H. Foulkes, and during some five years of this experience, and of many discussions on group analytic psychotherapy with Dr. Foulkes and his associates, I learnt a few simple skills that could be applied to teaching. The most important of these is listening, and the second is tolerating the expression of hostility in a relationship in which it is customarily suppressed. Something of what I owe to this experience for the development of a technique of conducting free group discussion will be apparent in Chapter 5.

The teaching project has been strongly influenced by another branch of study: recent research on visual perception. This emphasizes the part that our past experience and present attitude play in determining what we see, and its importance for observation in science is clear. Use was made in the experimental teaching course of some of the demonstrations of the projective nature of perception described in Chapters 2 and 3.

The teaching course that evolved was concerned with elucidating for the participants some of the factors that had affected their own judgment in scientific matters. The suggestion was that some understanding of how we make up our minds about what is seen in, say, radiographs, or about the interpretation of the results of an experiment, may help us to make more useful judgments about these and similar matters in the future. The judgment that any one person makes in getting information from a specific situation is of course only one of many possible alternatives. As the students discovered in discussion—often much to their surprise—several interpretations had been made of the same statement, or of the same radiograph. Potentially, many of the interpretations could have occurred to any one student, but he was usually not aware of any selecting process, and his choice of one interpretation rather than another was usually made more or less blindly.

My hypothesis is that we may learn to make better judgments if we can become aware of some of the factors that influence their formation. We may then be in a position to consider alternative judgments and to choose from among many instead of blindly and automatically accepting the first that comes; in other words, we may become more receptive, or mentally more flexible. The results of testing the effects of the course of discussions support this hypothesis.

The main difference between this and traditional methods of teaching is in the amount of attention that is paid to the *processes* of observing or thinking, as distinct from the results. In traditional teaching the student makes an observation, and finds it to be correct or incorrect by comparison with the teacher's (or the currently accepted) version. He learns by discovering disparities between his result and that obtained by more experienced and skilful persons. In the discussion technique of teaching, the student learns by comparing his observation with those of ten or so of his peers. He compares not only the results, but how the results were arrived at, and in doing this the range of factors taken into consideration is much wider than is usual in didactic teaching. What the student learns, it is hoped, is not only how to make a more correct response when he is confronted with a similar problem, but more generally to gain firmer control of his behaviour by understanding better his own ways of working.

The course consisted of eight discussions, each lasting about one and a half hours, and the students attended them in groups of twelve. The first three discussions were concerned with seeing, the fourth with language, the fifth with classification, the sixth with evaluation of evidence, the seventh with causation, and the eighth with reviewing the course. In the last three years we investigated the effect of the discussions by comparing the performance in observation tests of students who had taken the course with that of students otherwise similar, who had not yet taken it (James *et al.*, 1956). As described in Chapter 10, those students who had taken the course did significantly better than the others in four respects—they tended to discriminate better between facts and conclusions, to draw fewer false conclusions, to consider more than one solution to a problem, and to be less adversely influenced in their approach to a problem by their experience of a preceding one. That is, they were more objective and more flexible in their behaviour.

The anatomy of judgment

It is not intended, however, to give a detailed account of the course in this book, but to use my experience of it to illustrate some of the factors that affect scientific judgment. I chose 'The Anatomy of Judgment' as a title, because I propose to discuss the structure of scientific judgment as it can be understood by dissecting examples of making judgments in the class-room. The book is concerned not only with the structure of judgment but with its origin and development—how it comes to be as it is, how it is adapted to its function and in what conditions it can develop differently. This approach to the subject is one that comes most naturally to a biologist.

The book is divided into two parts. The first part gives a brief introduction to some aspects of the relation between the inner and outer worlds. It emphasizes the selective and interpretative nature of perception, and shows how the information that a person gets from a specified part of the outer world depends on the context, or total situation, and on his past experience, which is usefully thought of as being organized into schemata. Human relationships play an important role in perception both in that they are often a significant part of the context, and in that they have contributed to the formation, testing and modifying, of schemata.

In the second part I shall show how the principles of perception which have been outlined in the previous chapters apply to some of the processes involved in the formulation of scientific judgments by medical students. Each discussion reported here concerned the information that the various participants got from a specified part of the outer world (a radiograph for instance, or report of an experiment). By studying the different interpretations, it was possible to discover those factors of the context that had significantly contributed to them, and the kind of schemata that the students had used. During the discussions the students were mutually testing and modifying their schemata, and as a result of reorganizing their store of experience in this way were able later to make more valid interpretations. It is probable that the ways of thinking described here are commonly used by students of science, for only those schemata which were frequently used in the discussions are reported, and the topics that evoked them are of general importance to scientists.

The first part of the book can be considered as illustrating the schemata I used in dealing with the material of the second part—that is, in exploring students' ways of thinking, and helping to make them more effective.

Part One

THE RELATION BETWEEN
THE INSIDE AND OUTSIDE
WORLDS

2

Seeing Pictures

WE shall begin our study of how judgments are made by inquiring into some of the processes involved in getting information through seeing. Sight plays an extremely important role in the life of human beings, and is therefore interesting in itself, but, as we shall see, a study of some of the principles of visual perception serves also as a useful introduction to understanding how information is gained by other means. We shall begin with pictures, because examples are available to demonstrate the processes involved.

Interpreting

Most people, when they first look at Fig. 1, see a patchwork of black and white of no particular form. There will be on each retina of their two eyes an image of the picture, a dappling of light and shade, faithfully focused on to it by the lens and other transparent parts of the eye. Of the myriads of receptors in the retina some will receive light, those corresponding to the bright patches; others will receive less, or virtually none. And accordingly the nerve fibres running from the receptors to the brain will carry impulses that are relayed through a complicated network of channels in the central nervous system. The result of it all is that we are aware of a patchwork. The messages have been sent in the form of variations of electric potential in the nervous system and 'seeing' is a result of decoding, translating or interpreting these messages. In this particular case the result is that we get the information that there is a meaningless patchwork of black and white blotches.

The messages from the patchwork on the retina can, however, be interpreted in another way, as the head and shoulders of a man. Some people think the picture resembles a mediaeval representa-

Fig. 1. The Hidden Man. (*After P. B. Porter in The American Journal of Psychology,* vol. 67, p. 550, 1954)

tion of Christ. If you have not already seen the man he may appear if you look at the picture with the following description. His face is turned towards you, and occupies the middle third of the upper half of the picture. The top of the picture cuts across the brow so that the top of the head is not shown. The face is lit from the observer's right-hand side, so that the eyes are in shadow and the cheeks and chin brightly illuminated. His hair and beard are long, but the chin is clean shaven and is a white spot catching the light just above the middle of the picture. A white cloth covers the right shoulder and slopes across the breast; the left shoulder is turned a little away from you and the right upper sleeve is a black area in the lower left part of the picture.

The face may appear as suddenly as when a light has been switched on. Some people cannot see it with the help of words only, but need someone to trace the outline of the features over the patchwork. The object has not changed, nor has its image on the retina, yet the information received from the object is different—no longer is it seen as a chaotic patchwork, but as the picture of a man, sharp and clear and characteristic. (For those who still cannot 'see' it an explanatory drawing is given in Fig. 12 in the Appendix. See page 144.)

This demonstrates that what is perceived depends not only on what is being looked at but on the state of the perceiver. We can put this diagrammatically as in Fig. 2. The observer is at first in State 1, and looking at the object makes an interpretation; i.e., he receives Information A, namely that the picture is a jumble of black and white marks. Later he is in State 2, and looking at the same object he now makes a different interpretation, i.e., he receives Information B, namely that it is a picture of a man. The change of the observer from State 1 to State 2 may be the result of his having looked at the picture for some time, or of his having been given a verbal description of the man, or a sketched outline of his face. A few people may see the man immediately—that is, they are already in State 2. (An artist, for example, asked 'Why is it called The *Hidden* Man?') A few others may never see him—that is, they remain in State 1. Sometimes people fluctuate between States 1 and 2, alternately losing and finding the man, and sometimes after discovering him with great difficulty, they cannot be rid of him.

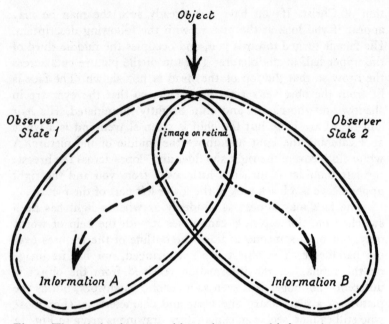

Fig. 2. The relation between object, observer and information received

Seeing the man has involved distinguishing certain marks which can stand for his features from others which can mean background; it has involved discrimination or judgment on the part of the observer. The verbal description, or the sketched outline, help us to make the discrimination, tell us what the marks can mean; in other words, they help us to interpret the pattern on the retina differently, thus getting different information from the picture. We tend to think of ourselves as passively receiving information from the outside world, but this is far from the case; in the process of receiving information we interpret and judge. I use these terms (in consultation with the Shorter Oxford and Webster's Dictionaries) in the following sense.

To interpret: to translate something which is obscure or ambiguous (e.g., a foreign language, or a dream) into intelligible terms.

To judge: to form an opinion; to estimate, infer, conclude, to make a judgment, i.e., to arrive at a decision or conclusion on the basis of indications and probabilities when the facts are not clearly ascertained.

The relation between the inner and outer worlds—in this case, between the picture and what we see—is a complex one. It is convenient to distinguish two points in the organism at which the information available is as it were sieved, and changed; at the sense organs, and at the nervous system. We are so familiar with the variations in sensitivity of different people's eyes that it is hardly necessary to draw attention to the selective action of the sense organs, which, according to their structure, can respond only to certain stimuli and not to others. We shall not be concerned with this aspect of selection of information, except to point out that the tools of the scientist, whether simple lens, telescope, electron microscope, thermometer, Geiger counter, sonograph or spectroscope, are designed to present to the eye information which is not otherwise available to it. In this book we shall be concerned with the results of the way the messages sent from the sense organs are dealt with by the central nervous system. It is possible that investigations of the mental equipment that scientists use in getting information, how they interpret and judge, will lead to advances just as great as have the improvements already effected in their laboratory equipment.

A part of our mental equipment that is concerned with receiving information and to which we shall devote some attention we shall refer to as a *schema*.

Schemata

When the Hidden Man appears it is as though he has suddenly fitted with a picture in our mind's eye. While people are trying to see him, and before they are given a description, they ask questions: what sort of a man? how big? in profile? as though they are searching for a picture in their mind's eye to match with him, to enable them to interpret the picture. It is as though they search for traces or impressions or models which past experiences have left, to which new experiences of sufficiently similar things can be matched or adapted. This introduces us to the useful notion of *schemata* which helps us to understand the relation of old and new information, and to think about how past experience predisposes an organism to behave in certain ways rather than in others. (See Oldfield and Zangwill, 1942, 1943, for the history of the concept, and Vernon, 1952, as illustrating its value in visual perception studies.) Bartlett (1932) defined a schema as 'an active organization of past reactions or of past experiences which must always be supposed to be operating in any well-adapted organic response'. Vernon (1955) has described schemata as 'persistent deep-rooted and well organized classifications of ways of perceiving, thinking and behaving', and Wolters (1943) stressed that the organizations are 'living and flexible'. It is unlikely that we shall ever have seen a portrait exactly like Fig. 1, but we have seen enough pictures of bearded men to give us a schema which helps us to interpret the black and white marks as a man's face. Schemata can be regarded as tools which help us to see, evaluate and respond.

Another example will show how schemata may help us *not* to see certain things. The schema into which the observer fits the new experience may be an inappropriate one.

Fig. 3. The Three Triangles. (Read the statement in each triangle.)
(*After* R. Brooks)

Most people read the statements in the triangles (Fig. 3) as 'Paris in the spring, Once in a lifetime, Bird in the hand' (Information A, Fig. 2). If they are urged to look again more carefully and to find out what is wrong, sooner or later they will see the extra words (Information B). When the observer was in State 1 a selection was made so that only those words that form the familiar phrases were seen; it is as though he was blind to the words which did not form part of this pattern, or as though he judged them to be irrelevant background. In State 2 he interprets the pattern on the retina in a different way. As with the 'Hidden Man' picture some people (for instance proof readers) are immediately in State 2, and others reach it only with great difficulty and after making conscious effort.

These examples emphasize the active role the observer plays

in organizing the information presented to him. We see how he uses his store of information in doing this. In the case of Fig. 1, when he cannot see the man, he fails to match the patchwork with any schema of a man; in the case of Fig. 3, when he fails to see the extra 'THE's' and 'A', he as it were distorts the pattern to fit the schemata of the well-known phrases. If his schemata are not sufficiently 'living and flexible', they hinder instead of help him to see.

This has been shown also for perception of colour and shape. The experiment (Bruner and Postman, 1949) was made with playing-cards, some of which had the colour changed, e.g., the six of clubs was red instead of black. The cards were exposed in succession for a very short time. Some of the subjects reported seeing normal cards instead of such anomalous cards; for example, they reported the red six of clubs as either a black six of clubs, or a red six of diamonds or hearts. Other subjects saw them as the six of clubs but purple or brown. Past experience of clubs (which were always black) had influenced the perception of clubs which in fact were red. It seems that rather than see such a monstrosity as a red club, people see what fits their schema, and will change the colour to what it 'ought' to be (black), or they will change the shape to fit the colour and call a club a diamond or heart, or they will compromise with brown or purple.

It was found that a shorter time of exposure of the cards was necessary to allow people to name the normal cards than the abnormally coloured ones. This fits in with much of our ordinary experience—that we see quickly and easily what we expect to see. Waiting in a bus queue we can distinguish the number of an approaching bus at a much greater distance if we know which numbers are likely to come along the road. Try the experiment of watching buses approach whose numbers you do not know with a friend who does. Let him say the number as soon as he recognizes it, when it is still a blur to you, and note how the number suddenly clarifies, almost it seems clicks into shape. In such cases when the thing we look at is sufficiently like the thing we expect to see, and easily fits our schema, our experience helps us to see. It is only when what we expect to see is not there that our schemata leads us astray.

How the schemata are used most effectively will depend on

what we want to achieve with them. Most newspapers contain printer's errors which the ordinary reader does not notice; and this is an advantage, because if he did notice them his attention would stray ineffectively from the subject matter of the article. On the other hand for proof-reading people train themselves to use such schemata as will help them to spot just those errors which the ordinary reader does better to ignore. Similarly, when editing it is usually easier to read a manuscript separately for sense and for style, using different kinds of schemata successively, rather than to try to use both simultaneously.

The effect of context

The Hidden Man and Three Triangles demonstrate that a visual pattern is interpreted differently according to the state of the observer, and hence according to which of his schemata he uses. They also demonstrate that, given a particular state of the observer, any one part of the pattern is interpreted in ways which depend on the rest of the pattern. The seeing of the face involves interpreting the patches at the sides of the face as background. The extra words are invisible because of the presence of others; if we wipe out the words around them, we cannot fail to see the extra 'THE's' and the extra 'A'.

Another example of the way parts of a pattern affect the interpretation of other parts is provided by Fig. 4. Here the three figures are of the same size but one feels certain that the man on the right is larger than the man on the left. The converging lines of the background lead one to think that the right-hand man is farther away than the others. In interpreting the picture of the right-hand man one has used information derived from his surroundings; that is, the context of the part attended to has affected its interpretation. We say that we react to the 'whole picture', even if we are concentrating attention on part of it only.

The effect of context can be demonstrated dramatically by cutting out two pieces of paper of identical size (about 7 inches long is suitable) shaped as in Fig. 5. In the position shown, A appears larger than B, but when A is placed to the right instead of the left of B, it appears smaller. That is to say, the apparent size of one piece depends on its position with regard to the other, and it can appear to swell or shrink as its position is changed.

When we are interpreting a stimulus pattern, isolatable parts of it which strongly affect our interpretation can be regarded as 'clues'. A clue guides us in the selection of a schema for the part attended to, and as soon as we have selected a schema, into which

Fig. 4. The Three Men.
(*After* Metzger)

a specific part fits, the rest becomes context or background. This ability to distinguish 'figure' from 'ground', to which the Gestalt psychologists have paid much attention, plays a very important part in perception (*see* Vernon, 1952). In the Three Men and The Two Shapes the clues are visual but, as with the Hidden Man, non-visual clues—for example, spoken words—may also affect the interpreting of a visual pattern. Remarks such as 'It is the head and shoulders of a man' or 'Don't you see any extra words?' may act as clues affecting the interpretation of Figs. 1 and 3.

Words and pictures

Two examples of experiments on the effect of non-visual clues may be cited. In the first (Carmichael, *et al.* 1932), people were shown a series of simple figures (Fig. 6, middle columns) each of which could represent, diagrammatically, two things. As each figure was shown, a suitable name was read out to one group of the subjects, an alternative name to the other. The two groups were then asked to draw what they had seen as accurately as possible. About a quarter of the drawings made (of which there were more than 3,000) differed markedly from the figures shown,

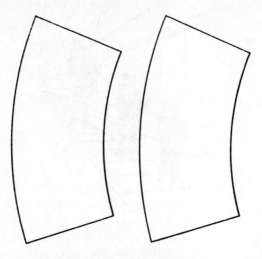

Fig. 5. The Two Shapes

and of these three-quarters approximated to the object whose name was given. It seems that the word given acts as a clue to help the observer select from all his schemata a suitable one into which to fit the pattern; according to which schema is selected, the pattern seen may be distorted to make a better fit.

Another experiment with more complicated materials has demonstrated that a story told before seeing a picture may affect how the picture is remembered (Davis and Sinha, 1950). The story concerned a feud between two neighbouring families, which culminated in the killing of the head of one of the families after a violent quarrel. The heir's wooing of the daughter of his father's murderer, and the wedding feast in conditions of tension, were described.

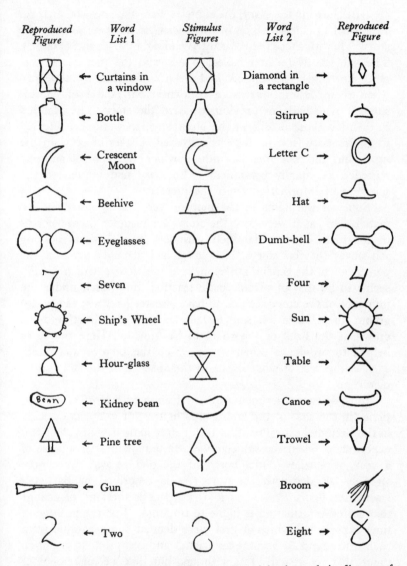

Reproduced Figure	Word List 1	Stimulus Figures	Word List 2	Reproduced Figure
	← Curtains in a window		Diamond in a rectangle →	
	← Bottle		Stirrup →	
	← Crescent Moon		Letter C →	
	← Beehive		Hat →	
	← Eyeglasses		Dumb-bell →	
	← Seven		Four →	
	← Ship's Wheel		Sun →	
	← Hour-glass		Table →	
	← Kidney bean		Canoe →	
	← Pine tree		Trowel →	
	← Gun		Broom →	
	← Two		Eight →	

Fig. 6. Ambiguous figures. (*After* L. Carmichael *et al.* in *Journ. of Experimental Psychology*, vol. 15, p. 80)

After hearing the story, the subjects were shown seven pictures and asked to choose which of them was the most relevant to the story. They all chose the 'Peasant Wedding' by Breughel (Plate I). The subjects were later asked to describe the picture. It was clear how their perception had been influenced by the story when their descriptions were compared with those of control subjects who had not previously heard the story. They tended to mention those details in the picture which were also referred to in the story (for instance, the crossed sheaves of corn on the wall), but did not mention others which the control subjects regarded as equally prominent. The story had influenced the selection of information from the picture.

Some of the items in the picture were falsely perceived, to match them, as it were with the story; for instance the musicians in the picture were identified with the 'two servants bearing ash-staves' of the story. The story had strongly affected the perception of the general atmosphere of the picture, which usually seems to be that of placid rustic feasting, but which under the influence of the story seemed to have sinister features; the bride-groom for instance was said to look 'sad and downcast' and the crowd at the back of the room to be 'unruly'. Here the story helped to provide a schema into which the picture was fitted, even at the cost of what seems in the absence of the story to be distortion.

In these two experiments we are dealing with *recall* of perceptions; in the case of the ambiguous figures, of immediate recall, in the Breughel experiment, of recall after some days. In the latter experiments when the subjects were tested again after a lapse of a year, what they remembered of the picture was even more strongly blended with the story. As is described in Bartlett's fascinating book, *Remembering* (1932), this is the kind of change that stored information is liable to undergo. With the passage of time experiences which at first were defined and separable from each other tend to become associated and confused. It is not so much that we actually forget things, but that we misremember them; the memory, for many events, is not so much a sieve as a melting-pot. Schemata may continually change, blend with and modify each other.

From the point of view of everyday life, the way we perceive

Kunsthistorisches Museum

PLATE I. Peasant Wedding (Breughel)

things as it were in retrospect is very important, for we are continually acting on *stored* information, that is, on interpretations of patterns which have already left the retina. This may have happened only a fraction of a second before, as when we cross the road having just looked over our shoulder at an approaching car, or it may have happened long ago, as when we find our way about a town that we revisit after an absence of many years.

In the case of the Three Triangles or the Ambiguous Figures the schemata that the observer uses are fairly well prescribed and definite. One can think of them as traces or models of things previously seen, as though the phrase 'Paris in the Spring', if seen often enough, leaves a kind of imprint on the mind's eye, into which the phrase in the triangle must be made to fit. In this case the observer autonomously supplies the schema. In the case of the Ambiguous Figures, we saw how the choice of schemata was determined by words spoken by the experimenter. Many of the schemata that affect our behaviour are of a much more generalized and diffuse kind than these examples, and how we use them is determined by the complex of schemata which together determine what we call 'attitude'.

I shall now give an example of the same picture being differently interpreted by different people according to the views they hold as to how the artist made the picture, that is, the choice of schemata used was determined autonomously by the general attitude of the observer to works of art. It has a special moral for those interested in seeing in scientific work, so I shall discuss it at some length.

The case of the cave paintings

Two widely different interpretations of certain cave paintings have been put forward. The conventional view of these is that the artists depicted the animals in lively action. The great student of cave art, the Abbé Breuil, wrote (1952) that 'the Quarternary artist . . . knew how to seize the different animal attitudes, some- times simply standing resting, sometimes lying down or stretching, sometimes strolling lazily, sometimes galloping.' Such titles as 'the bellowing bison', the 'trotting boar', 'the charging mammoth' are commonly given to the pictures. It is supposed that the artists were hunters who became so familiar with the behaviour of the animals in the field that they were able to take back to the caves 'snapshots' in their mind's eye of the beasts in characteristic poses, which they rendered in paint with extraordinary skill. Luquet (1923), for instance, wrote: *Si nous passons des groupes aux figures d'animaux isolés, on pourrait en citer un grand nombre dont l'attitude ou le mouvement est rendu avec un vérité dénotant une observation attentive de la nature, ce qui n'a rien de surprenant chez des chasseurs.*

Comparison of some of the cave paintings with photographs of living mammals may seem at first glance to support this view. For instance, the general impressions of the animals in Plate II (a) and (b) are very similar. Plate II (a) is from the Altamira caves and Breuil described it thus: 'A pair of male bison; these are tail to tail and their powerful dark brown silhouettes stand out well. Each is scampering away in an opposite direction.' Plate II (b) for comparison is a photograph of rapidly moving wildebeest in Northern Rhodesia. Again, in Plate III (a) the 'swimming stags' of the Altamira caves look very like the migrating reindeer photographed in Lapland (III (b)) (although they could also be just the heads and shoulders of standing or lying stags, since no background is painted).

However, Leason, an artist (1939, 1956), offered an alternative explanation of the cave drawings as being painstaking representations of carcases lying on the ground. He had chanced to make drawings looking down at a cat and a snake which had killed each other and remarked how vigorous the cat looked. He said that when he 'first saw reproductions of Quaternary cave art, it struck him as a remarkable fact that these artists of so many thousand years ago should have made direct studies of dead animals! It never occurred to him that any other interpretation could be placed upon the pictures which bore none of the titles suggesting action, now given to them in archaeological literature.' In a very interesting and amusing paper Leason gives tracings of photographs of various dead animals for comparison with some of the cave paintings (Fig. 7).

He notes that many features of the paintings—the position of the feet, the tail, the tongue hanging out—resemble those of carcases with muscles relaxed in death. He contrasts the realistic treatment of the head, which must indicate acute observation, with the failure to make the feet look as though they are supporting

H. Breuil

Nigel Watt

PLATE II. Cave paintings and live animals
Above: Cave painting of bison, Altamira
Below: Wildebeest, Northern Rhodesia

S. *Gillsäter*

PLATE III. Cave paintings and live animals
Above: Cave painting of 'swimming stags', Altamira
Below: Migrating reindeer, Lapland

the weight of the body. Referring to the 'bellowing bison' of Altamira he says that 'the spectacle of some farmyard cow rising lightly on all four hoof tips and emitting a bellow, is too much for the imagination,' and continues: 'Few, if any, of the other animals in this Altamira frieze maintain what could strictly be called normal contact with the earth. Of twenty-five standing and seemingly moving beasts represented in the colour plates of Breuil's publication not more than two or three suggest that they would have left normal footprints when they passed on; and even

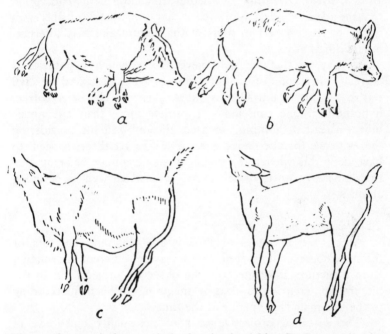

Fig. 7. Cave paintings and dead animals. (*After* P. Leason in the *Proceedings of the Prehistoric Society*, N.S.5, p. 51, 1939.) Tracings from the Abbé Breuil's drawings of Altamira cave paintings (*a, c*); and from photographs of dead animals (*b, d*).

(*a*) A 'trotting boar'.
(*b*) A slaughtered pig. A composite tracing from two photographs, with legs in different positions.
(*c*) A 'bellowing bison'.
(*d*) A dead sambur hind.

these raise some doubt as to whether their tracks would not have appeared strange to hunters well versed in their ways.'

The difference of opinion about the cave paintings illustrates very clearly the effect of the general attitude of the observer on how he interprets a picture. The protruding tongues, the anomolous position of the feet, the absence of attempt to show background, the fact that the figures are seldom composed in natural groups were noticed by proponents of the live art theory, but they interpreted them differently from Leason (see, for instance, Brown, 1928). According to whether they have the preconception that the artists' models were alive or that they were dead, observers notice or neglect certain parts of the picture and may interpret others differently.

It may be that we shall never know which hypothesis is correct; but a point of scientific interest arises here, and we shall return to this again. One is more likely to choose a correct hypothesis if one consciously considers more than one possibility instead of 'jumping to a conclusion' without considering the evidence for alternative ones. The live art theorists seem to have done this whereas Leason had the advantage of being able to compare two sets of schemata, of dead as well as of living animals.

The projective nature of perception

All of these examples which show that different observers, or the same observer at different times, may get different information from a picture, illustrate how the observer 'projects' on to the picture, i.e., contributes ideas or imaginings of his own according to the schemata that operate at the time.

The so-called projective tests of personality make use of pictures which stimulate fantasy, so that what people say they see reveals (to those trained to understand) a great deal about their general attitude or frame of mind, that is, the kind of schemata they commonly use. One of the best known of these is the Rorschach inkblot test, an example of which is shown in Plate IV.

These pictures were made by putting a blob of ink on a piece of paper and folding the paper over it so that a symmetrical smudge of colour is formed. The patterns are thus 'meaningless' in the sense that the person who made them did not intend to represent anything; nevertheless people do see things in them, and may feel quite strongly about what they see.

We may, then, regard pictures as lying in a kind of continuum. At one end there will be drawings, realistic paintings and photographs that are representational. For all practical purposes most of us interpret these in the same way most of the time, the interpretation being comparatively little affected by extraneous circumstances. The pictures easily fit into our schemata of similar things with which we are familiar. At the other, the fantasy end, will be inkblots or pictures in the fire or in clouds, or non-representational paintings which different people, and the same person at different times, may interpret very variously. Such patterns may fit into one of several schemata so that many interpretations may be made.

Now it is important to note that some pictures would be at one end of the continuum for some observers and at the opposite end for others. For most people Plate V will be at the fantasy end, meaning as little, or as much, as an inkblot, but for others it will be at the representational end. People appropriately trained in interpretation of radiographs will recognize it as a radiograph of part of a human head, taken through the chin and nape of neck, matching the picture with their schemata of radiographs of human heads. This introduces us to the importance of training in perception, and how we learn to see.

3

Learning to See

WE cannot avoid recognizing that a certain amount of training is necessary to understand pictures, for it is only too clear that many of us do not understand modern art. Many paintings now acceptable to us (judging by how frequently they are reproduced) were ignored or ridiculed when first exhibited. It is perfectly clear also, that training is necessary to interpret radiographs. It is not so easily apparent, however, that we have had to learn to see ordinary things, because seeing seems to be an effortless process. You are not aware of doing any hard work, or of exercising any skill, in distinguishing your mother from your father, a square from a circle, in recognizing that your nose is closer to your eye than your foot is, or a tree-top nearer than the moon. 'The perceptual act is not an *activity*. There is no element of fussiness, no wondering or questioning, one does not have to take trouble over it—it is a blessed relief from the labour of discursive thought' (Price, 1932).

As a matter of fact, however, each of us has had to learn to see ordinary things, to develop and exercise a skill of seeing. Most of us did this in infancy as a part of natural development, and we have forgotten how much effort it cost us. Some acute students of child behaviour have said that a two-and-a-half-year-old child 'may sometimes look with such overpowering intensity that his legs collapse under him' (Gesell *et al.*, 1949). Studies of adults congenitally blind because of cataract, who were able to see after operation, have shown that learning to see is for them an extraordinarily complex and laborious process. Schemata are built up slowly. It took at least a month for a patient to learn to distinguish even a small number of objects as other people do. After thirteen days of training, a patient could not say what was the difference between a square and a triangle without counting the corners. Although a cube of sugar could be correctly named when seen on the table it was not recognized when suspended by a thread against a different background (Senden, 1932).

The need for prolonged apprenticeship in seeing has also been demonstrated by some experiments on chimpanzees which were reared in darkness up to the age of sixteen months. Apart from eye reflexes, which were normal, the animals behaved as though they were blind for some time after they had been brought into daylight. For instance, if the nipple of a feeding-bottle touched the hand or face, it was immediately seized by the mouth, but there was no sign of visual recognition of it until the thirty-third meal taken on the eleventh day after the animal had been brought into daylight (Riesen, 1947).

The work of Ames

To the great volume of recent work which has increased our understanding of how we learn to see, Ames (1955) and his colleagues (e.g., Kilpatrick, 1952; Ittelson and Cantril, 1954) have made contributions which we shall find specially useful to quote here. I shall refer first to some experiments on the perception of size.

When people are shown playing-cards of different sizes in an otherwise darkened room, they do not see them as differing in size, but as being at distances which vary inversely with their size. If a normal card, one half as big, and another twice as big, are placed at the same distance, the observer sees them all as normal cards, the small one more distant, the large one nearer, than the normal one. Thus the observer alters the distance at which the cards appear to be placed in order to make all playing-cards conform to his schema of the standard-size cards with which he is familiar.

Ames and his co-workers explain this phenomenon in terms of 'assumptions' which the observer learns to make about the nature of playing-cards. An assumption is defined as a weighted average of previous experiences, and for my purposes can be taken as equivalent to a schema. Most playing-cards are of a standard size and shape, and as a result of using them we learn to make assumptions as to the size and shape of all playing-cards.

The image which a playing-card makes on the retina (which may be imitated by suitable optical arrangements of lenses and screen to represent the eye) varies according to its position relative to the eye. The size of the image will vary with distance, and its shape will be much more often trapezoidal than rectangular.

When we are playing a game of cards, the sizes and shapes of the images of the cards are continually changing; even if the cards are lying still their images on the retina change with the slightest movement of our head. But we learn to interpret these differing images and assume a constant size and shape for the playing-cards. Every time we put out our hand to pick up a card, we are both using our assumptions as to its size and shape to determine its position, and testing them. If we are able to pick up a card we have proved our assumptions to be correct. In this way, if we play with standard cards long enough, we learn to make verifiable assumptions on which we can base effective action.

In ordinary circumstances such assumptions are useful because they help us to see quickly and easily. But if we are presented with non-standard cards, we may go on using the assumptions we learned to make for standard cards and thus be led astray. For instance, if in the experiment cited above, the person who is shown playing-cards of different sizes tries to touch them, he cannot do so. He will not stretch far enough when he tries to touch the larger card which he thinks is near and he will stretch too far when he tries to touch the smaller one. His assumptions are not useful in these conditions, and if he is to act effectively he must modify them. If his assumptions are not modifiable he is unable to take in the new piece of information—that the playing-cards are of non-standard size; he cannot see such cards as the size they 'really' are, nor at their correct distance. If abnormal cards are seen often enough in suitable circumstances the assumptions about cards will change. As long as our assumptions are not challenged when we act on them, we shall keep them fixed. If we do not try to touch the cards, we shall go on seeing them at the wrong distance.

One of the most remarkable of Ames's demonstrations is that of the 'distorted room' (Fig. 8 and Plate VI). This is a room which, when viewed through a peephole in one wall, looks like an ordinary symmetrical room with two similar windows at the far side. It

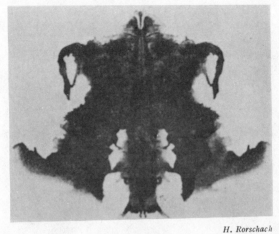

H. Rorschach

PLATE IV. Inkblot

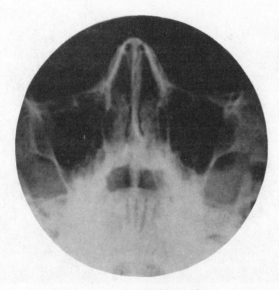

PLATE V. Radiograph

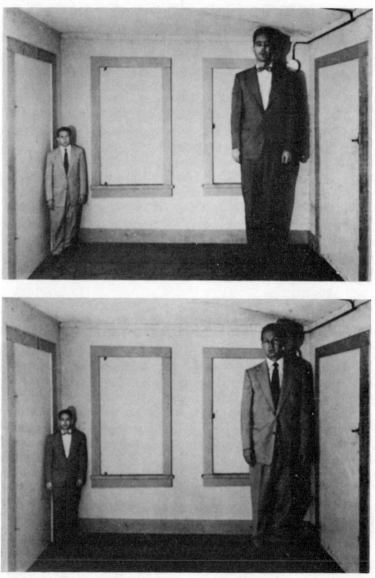

E. P. Kilpatrick

PLATE VI. The Distorted Room

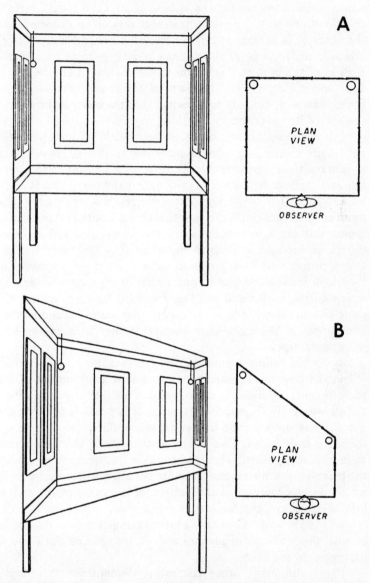

Fig. 8. The Distorted Room. (*After* Earl C. Kelley in *Education for What is Real*, Harper and Brothers.) *Above:* The room as it appears. *Below:* The room as it is

seems to the observer that he is looking into the room from the middle of one wall. The room is in fact very much distorted, and the observer is peeping into it not from the centre point but from one side of it. None of the corners is a right-angle; one of the corners of the back wall is nearer to the observer than the other; floor and ceiling slope. The parts of the room, windows, floor cover, wainscot, etc., are so designed that the room looks normal in spite of its queer shape.

For instance, the windows are trapezoidal and the one in the right-hand corner is smaller than the one in the left, so although it is actually nearer to the observer it seems to be of the same size and at the same distance as the right-hand one which is really larger and farther away. The retinal images of all the parts of the room are consistent with the view that this is a normal symmetrical room, and one's assumptions are not challenged unless other things are brought into the room, when they look very strange. When people who have not been built to fit the room come in, they look incongruous, and appear tiny or gigantic according to which corner they stand in. The room makes them appear the same distance away, whichever corner they stand in, and so they look larger in the right-hand (nearer) corner than in the left, more distant one.

A marble rolling across the floor may appear to go uphill. When the observer is asked to try to follow a toy mouse with a stick he finds it difficult to do so, because his estimates of position are all wrong. With practice, however, it is possible to catch the mouse, that is, to decode the retinal image differently and to see the room as distorted. This is apparently done by using clues that were formerly ignored, which, when taken into account, give away the true shape of the room. There are certain features of the room which do not conform to the pattern of a normal room, and at first these discrepant features are not seen. They are like the extra 'THE's' and 'A' in the Three Triangles which do not fit in with the well-known phrases and so are ignored until one is prompted to see them.

These and many other fascinating demonstrations indicate the extremely complex nature of the processes involved in seeing ordinary things. Whether it is a three-dimensional thing that is looked at, or a picture of a thing, it is its retinal image that is interpreted. The Hidden Man has demonstrated that different information may be got on different occasions from the same retinal image. Ames and his co-workers (Kilpatrick, 1952) have elegantly demonstrated that the same information may be got from different things if the images they throw on the retina are sufficiently alike.

In this demonstration (Fig. 9) the subject looks through three peepholes, *a*, *b*, and *c*, in a screen and each time he sees a chair.

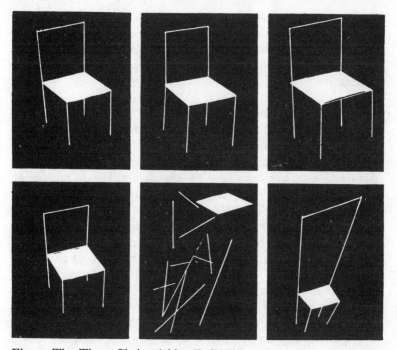

Fig. 9. The Three Chairs. (*After* F. P. Kilpatrick.) *Above:* What the observer sees through the peepholes. *Below:* What he sees behind the screen

The three chairs look alike, of a certain size and in a certain position. When he goes behind the screen, however, he sees three different things, none of them chairs. What he looked at through peephole *a*, consisted of a piece of cardboard and a set of strings arranged in the form of a chair. Through peephole *b*, he looked at a set of strings of different lengths and arranged at different angles, and a white diamond painted on the wall at the back. Through the third peephole he looked at a set of strings and a piece of cardboard arranged to make a perspective projection of a chair-shaped object.

The difference between a chair and these false chairs is that the chair continues to look like a chair when viewed from many different aspects; it will stand up to the test of getting information from it in different ways. The others will not. The image they cast on the retina when the eye is at the peephole will be so similar to that cast by a chair that it will be interpreted as such; but the image they cast on the retina when the eye is in any other position will be so dissimilar from that of a chair, that it will be interpreted differently.

Selection from the store of information

That we select from the stimulus pattern has already been amply demonstrated—most clearly perhaps in the Three Triangles —but we have not so far emphasized sufficiently that a selection is also made from our own store of information. We do not use all those parts of our store of information which might be useful. In reading the Three Triangles for instance we do not use our knowledge that printers sometimes make mistakes. In the distorted room the observer first sees the room normal and the people distorted; that is, he uses his schemata of the shape of rooms but not his schemata of the size of people—he has selected from his own store of information.

At first the observer sees the room as normal and the people distorted in size (information A), having selected certain parts of the stimulus pattern (chiefly those which are the same as a normal room's image), and certain parts of his own store of information (chiefly those schemata concerning the shape of normal rooms). After having practised using information A and found that it does not help him to behave effectively, he makes a different selection from the stimulus pattern (now perceiving the parts which are not consistent with those of a normal room) and a different selection from his own store of information (now using schemata of the size of people which were neglected before) and consequently makes a different interpretation, receiving information B, that the room is distorted and the people normal. This experience has added new pieces of information to the observer's store of information; he now knows that rooms which are distorted can look normal.

The question still arises why the first selection was made at first in preference to the second—why should the people who are normal look wrong and the room that is really distorted look normal? Why has he made this particular selection and not the alternative? Why does the presence of normal people not make the observer see the room for what it is, distorted? A likely explanation is that we need to keep our environment stable. We easily get upset and seasick if the world seems to move around us. Our ability to estimate distances correctly, by interpreting trapezoidal images as rectangles in perspective for instance, is of the greatest importance to us in moving safely about the world and getting what we need. When we are forced to admit incongruity we prefer to see it in movable objects like people rather than in static ones like rooms.

Incidentally this is not so for everyone looking into the room. It was found that a certain woman saw her husband, but not other people, as normal and the room distorted, and further investigation showed that this was the case with several newly married people. One might suppose that they were particularly anxious that their new spouses should remain as they knew them to be. Thus we interpret the stimulus pattern in terms of our past experience and present and future needs.

Going beyond the information presented

So far we have referred to assumptions and schemata as though they are mainly visual; but they are clearly very complex. Our schemata of apples, for instance, are compounded of impressions received by many sense organs, of colour, shape, size and texture as seen with the eyes; shape, size and texture, coolness and weight as felt by the hands; texture and coolness by the teeth and tongue; smell and taste; the rattle of the pips when shaken or the crunch when bitten detected by the ear.

When these complex schemata are used appropriately, we can take for granted a lot of other properties about which we have no direct evidence at the moment. When, for instance, we choose by sight what we think is the best apple from a dishful, we receive visually certain information about its size, shape and colour, and we choose that particular apple because we think it will taste nicer than the others. This means that we are going beyond the information immediately given (extrapolating or predicting) by using our complex of schemata of apples, not only our visual one; we are assuming that the apple has other properties, for example, a certain relation of sugar to acid content, a certain texture, which we have not yet been able to perceive, and it is for these properties that the apple is desirable.

We may, of course, find that our schemata have failed to allow us to predict correctly. Those of us who grew up before man-made fibres were widely used learned how to judge by sight woollen socks for future wear and washing. When we first meet with spun nylon socks that look like wool, and even feel like wool, we may expect them to behave like wool. But if we use nylon socks often enough we learn not only to make a set of useful expectations about socks we are reliably informed are of nylon, but also to detect the differences visually and tactually ourselves, between nylon and wool. At first we may say we had the same visual and tactual schema for nylon as for wool; later we acquire two different ones. We are thus continually learning to see by the very process of acting on what we see.

The radiologist acquires his skill in just the same way, by learning to relate the present visual pattern to the relevant complex of schemata in such a way that he can safely extrapolate and predict. We said (page 39 Plate V) that a radiograph could be at the fantasy end of the continuum of pictures for laymen and at the representational end for a radiologist. A radiologist differs from laymen in having seen many radiographs, so that he has built up visual schemata of them. But he differs also in that he knows (as laymen do not) how to get other information about the things shown in the radiograph; he correlates certain shadows with the results of other investigations of the patient—his state of health, or reaction to clinical tests for instance. He can therefore check whether a shadow which fits his schemata of say, tubercular lesions, indicates that the patient has tuberculosis. This is comparable with going behind the screen in the Three Chairs demonstration, to find whether all the information you can get from them fits in with your schemata of chairs, or only parts of it.

Seeing and touching

It is not necessary to emphasize the enormous restrictions that blindness imposes upon the ordinary procedures of getting a living: we are only too well aware that we are in general more dependent on sight than on smell, touch or hearing (and in this we differ from many other animals). But it is worth pointing out that sight affects the knowledge of the world we receive through our other senses.

It is well known that other senses may be exceptionally well developed in blind people. For instance, Laura Bridgman, the famous blind deaf-mute, could recognize, after a year's interval, the hand of a person who had once shaken hers; and Julia Brace is said to have been employed sorting by smell the newly washed linen belonging to numerous inmates of an institution (Gibson, 1953). It might be supposed that the knowledge the blind have of the world through touch would be of the same kind but better, more detailed, than ours, and that they could for instance, make models, which are accurate according to our standards, of objects they know by feel. But though there have been several blind sculptors whose work is well regarded it seems that none of these was blind from birth. People who have always been blind make models of, e.g., heads which to us look distorted, and what they say about sculptured busts which they examine by touch does not conform with what we perceive. Revesz (1950) therefore considered that there are two senses of touch: of the blind and of the sighted. In people who have both senses, sight and touch are inextricably confounded. A sculptor who was blind-folded did not recognize by touch a bust which had stood within sight of her desk for years.

It would seem then that to the blind, especially to those who have been blind from birth, the world of touch is very different from the world of those who see and even of the blind who have seen for a short time in earliest childhood. Their schemata have been built up from different evidence. The famous cases of a few blind people who had exceptional talents and educational opportunities tend to blur these differences. The reports that

Helen Keller (1914) gives of her world, for instance, show that her schemata were profoundly influenced by what she had learned from verbal descriptions of other people's sensations. She 'saw' through what other people said they had seen.

Seeing people

We cannot so easily perfect our schemata of people as of those of apples or socks. As we know only too well we do not all agree about what we see and we often fail to predict correctly a person's behaviour. According to their past experience and future intentions one person sees a policeman as a kindly figure who safeguards his passage across the road, another sees him as an enemy who may send him to the law-courts.

Apart from differences in interpretation according to the schemata employed in perceiving people, there is a further source of confusion; in interpersonal situations the observer influences the other persons he observes. The way in which I look at a table does not affect the table; whether I look at it with a frown or a smile the image it throws on my retina will be the same (though, as we have seen, the information I get from it may well be different, according to my state as I interpret it). By contrast, whether I look at my son or my husband with a smile or a frown certainly does affect them, and consequently changes the image which the light rays coming from them makes on my retina (or on anybody else's for that matter).

Similarly, the policeman referred to above may in fact behave differently if he believes that the observer needs help to cross the road because of infirmity or because of inebriation. So intimate and indissociable are the relations between the participants in the perceptual act that in some cases we can be said to make our predictions come true, as when he who thinks himself unloved behaves in such a way as to make it difficult for anyone to love him. Such a person is caught in a hopelessly closed vicious circle, because his schemata of people's behaviour· are continually reinforced by receiving confirmatory information; he cannot be presented with contradictory information until his own behaviour influences people differently. Small wonder then, that in personal relations the information we obtain from a given visual pattern is not always such as will lead to the most effective way of behaving, even when it does allow correct prediction.

Seeing new relationships

The tendency in seeing to ignore or reject what does not fit in with the pattern expected has been illustrated by the Three Triangles. G. H. Lewes (1879) expressed this admirably when he said: 'And the new object presented to Sense, or the new idea presented to Thought, must also be *soluble in old experiences*, be *re*-cognized as like them, otherwise it will be unperceived, uncomprehended.' Many examples from common life can be given. Children play a kind of game which might be called 'Do as I do'. There are very many varieties, but basically the leader challenges the victims to imitate him as, for instance, he outlines a face on the floor, chanting 'Two eyes a nose and a mouth. Do as I do'. The victims hopefully follow the leader's actions but they do not pass the test, for the pattern they have seen and copied is only part of the pattern that he has ordained shall be copied. He may have coughed or crossed his arms or scratched his ear in addition to outlining the face, and his victims fail because they do not appreciate this as part of the instructions.

Successful detectives differ from less successful ones in their ability to perceive as relevant to the solution of their problem, pieces of information which the rest of us ignore, regard as irrelevant, do not see. In a story by G. K. Chesterton, *The Invisible Man*, it was known that a man intended to commit murder, and four men were set to watch the house in which his victim lived. When questioned as to what persons had entered the house, they said no one. The murder had been committed by a postman, who had been 'mentally invisible' because they had seen his visit as relevant to the customary delivery of mail and as irrelevant to the unusual event of crime.

Diagnosis in medicine is a kind of detective work and the following is an example where a doctor at first did not regard a piece of information as relevant to the solution of his problem. A child with a persistent cough had its throat X-rayed for diagnosis. The radiologist reported that there was nothing in the radiograph to show why the child was coughing. The cough persisted, and the child returned to have another radiograph taken. This time the shadow of a button was seen in the throat region, the button was removed and the child stopped coughing.

When the first radiograph was re-examined the shadow of the button was seen there too, but the radiologist had explained it away to himself, supposing that the child had been X-rayed with its vest on. He had failed to see the significance of the button for the problem in hand—diagnosis of the cause of the cough—because another explanation for its presence seemed more probable. After all, most people wear their buttons outside and not inside their throats, just as most postmen deliver letters and not death.

Important discoveries in science provide clear examples of the scientist making new use of information which had previously been regarded as unimportant or useless. We may cite, for example, the well-known case of Fleming's observation, which led some years later to the discovery of penicillin. Fleming was growing cultures of bacteria and noticed that in some cases the culture was eroded away. Such a thing must have occurred many times before, but was not followed up; it was regarded as having relevance only to the growing of bacteria in cultures. Fleming, however, saw its relevance to the prevention of growth of bacteria within the body. Instead of throwing such eroded cultures away, he kept them and grew the mould which prevented the growth of bacteria.

Inventiveness or imagination in science then depends on the possibility of making new associations of schemata, especially of those that were not developed in close association and that consequently have no conventional or traditional relationships.

Seeing without knowing

The Three Triangles give us an example of a kind of unconscious refusal to see a word which can be clearly visible. We turn now to consider cases where we behave as though we have unconsciously seen something which is invisible.

A famous example of a visual illusion is the Müller-Lyer lines (Fig. 10); the lines *a* and *b* are equal in length but *a* looks shorter than *b*. The presence of the little lines at their ends, in one case directed towards each other, in the other away from each other, makes one line look longer than the other. Now if these little lines are made so faint that they are just not visible for most people, *a* and *b* still look a different length (Dunlap, 1900; Bressler, 1931). That is to say, something we are not able to see consciously has affected our judgment. This example differs from the Three Men in that the lines that affect our judgment of the size of the men are clearly visible, though we may not pay attention to them.

There is now a great deal of evidence that we react in complicated ways to visual stimuli which we not only seem not to notice, but which we cannot see in the ordinary sense of the word,

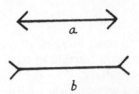

Fig. 10. The Müller-Lyer illusion.

even if we try to (Miller, 1951). We shall not pursue this fascinating topic further than to suggest that such unconscious perception may play an important role in many highly developed skills such as those involved in medical diagnosis, and that the possibility of extending our conscious control into these unlit areas of behaviour might be investigated with profit.

The language of perception

There are various ways of expressing the fact that we never come to an act of perception with an entirely blank mind, but are always in a state of preparedness or expectancy, because of our past experience. The terms *schema* as used above, *assumptions* as used by Ames and his co-workers, *hypotheses* as used by Bruner (1951) and *brain models* by Young (1951) are examples. Hebb (1949), attempting to combine findings of psychology and neurology, has postulated the development of 'cell-assemblies' in the brain as a conceptual tool for dealing with perception, learning and expectancy. These are diffuse sets of pathways which develop as a result of repeated stimulation of a given kind, and may interact with each other, in a fashion analogous with schemata.

The use of these and other terms to describe the state of

readiness in which the perceiver comes to any act of perception, their changing meanings and subtle implications, and their inter-action with the ways of thinking of the workers using them, is a fascinating study in itself. The word 'schema' is useful for describing experience organized in fairly well-defined patterns (for example, the schema of bearded men's faces). For loose associations of schemata—that is, for experience organized in more generalized, vague or ill-defined patterns, such as 'attitude to sex'—the term 'assumption' seems more appropriate (Ames, however, uses 'assumption' for both well-defined and vague patterns).

In this brief introduction to some of the processes involved in seeing, only a very small fraction of the knowledge at present available has been considered. My conscious aim in selecting from this rich field was to take only what seemed to be relevant to the problems of observing accurately and comprehensively in biological studies. Much of what I seem to have ignored un-doubtedly affected the information I received, and undoubtedly much that is plain to other observers is concealed from me because of the limitations of my schemata.

4

Human Relations in Getting Information

IN the Introduction reference was made to two recent branches of study, visual perception and group psychotherapy, which have greatly influenced the project described in this book. Chapters 2 and 3 have dealt with the first, and have discussed some of the factors that affect our perception of the external world, but this was done with almost complete disregard of the biological fact that man is a social animal. The reader may well wonder what part could be played in the project by group psychotherapy, which is entirely concerned with the relationships of people to each other. This chapter shows how human relationships influence the receipt of information even about apparently non-personal events.

In the beginning
From the very beginning of a child's life human relationships play an important part in the building of schemata. There is considerable evidence that a baby's intelligence suffers if it is not mothered enough (Bowlby, 1951). The early establishment of a warm and constant relationship with a mother or mother substitute seems to be essential for the normal development not only of behaviour in fields not commonly regarded as concerned with social behaviour, which is what one might expect, but also of human relationships. A study of the intelligence of children who were not brought up by their own parents has been made by Goldfarb (1943). The intelligence quotients of children brought up in an institution were lower than those of similar children brought up by foster-parents in ordinary family home conditions. Their capacity for abstract thinking was seriously impaired.

Some experiments on dogs illustrate that they too are strongly

55

affected by the psychological environment in which they are reared. Puppies treated as pets of the family showed more mature patterns of behaviour than their siblings brought up in isolation in laboratory cages and their capacity to solve problems was greater (Bindra, 1956). It seems that the effects of sensory deprivation in the early months of life are permanent. The implications of this work for education generally are of the greatest importance.

Further light on what makes people behave the way they do comes from the work done at McGill University (Bexton *et al*, 1954), sometimes colourfully referred to as the 'coffin experiments'. These showed that normal intelligent behaviour requires a continually varied sensory input; the brain works properly only if it is kept continually 'warmed up'. In these experiments students were paid twice as much as they could earn in other jobs to lie in a comfortable bed in a lighted and partly sound-proofed cubicle. They wore translucent goggles so that no clear images were seen. They could communicate by telephone to the experimenters, to ask for food, etc., but otherwise had no contact with the outside world and nothing to do.

Some subjects stayed in this isolation for as long as forty-eight hours. They tended to become restless and irritable; some had headaches and nausea; and some could not stand the experience and left in spite of the high rate of pay. Some became confused and even hallucinated. One man described his experience of seeing a procession of squirrels with sacks over their shoulders marching purposefully across a snowfield. But from the point of view of intellectual behaviour the most interesting finding was that the ability to do problem-solving tests was lowered—the students became more stupid as a result of isolation and sensory deprivation.

It seems then that any sensory event has two effects. It acts as a cue which gives rise to a specific response, and it helps to arouse the system in general, to make it vigilant as it were to cues (Hebb, 1955). The 'natural' ways mothers have of treating a baby, of fondling it, cooing at it and chucking it under the chin, have as 'cue' function the elicitation of a gurgle of delight, which pleases the mother. But perhaps their 'arousal' function is much more important and more permanent in its effects, in tuning up the growing nervous system so that it reacts appropriately to other stimulation from the environment.

Culture and communication

In the earliest months of life, then, one of the most important factors which affect the building of schemata is the behaviour of the mother and other people who come into close physical contact with the infant. Later, an important part of our store of information is taken in as it were by the pores of the skin from the wider culture in which we live. We naturally absorb a number of attitudes, or behaviour patterns—i.e., complexes of schemata or assumptions which are shared in common with the people around us who were similarly brought up, and which are different from those of other social units, other nations, or other classes within nations. It is the job of the parents and teachers to instruct children in the accepted customs and regulations of a given society, so that they can live harmoniously in it. Some of this instruction is done verbally, as with the Ten Commandments, or rules about which side of the road one may drive on. But much of it is transmitted non-verbally, by example from those already indoctrinated, as in posture and manner of walking, which are different in our culture for boys and for girls.

In periods of stability or of slow change the broad outlines of the pattern of the culture are accepted by the majority almost unthinkingly and without challenge, and the principles that should govern behaviour are so thoroughly inculcated that they hardly need verbal reinforcement or even expression. The relationships between the sexes, of children to parents, of the able-bodied to the sick or elderly, are of this kind; they have been established by custom and are automatically followed by the majority, and their rejection by the few is visited with guilt and, if sufficiently apparent, with social ostracism. Much of the body of culture is thus received from a source which is effectively anonymous; in the form of religion or folklore it is passed on as a dogma not to be questioned (Ruesch and Bateson, 1951).

In the same way it is extremely difficult for scientists to question the basic assumptions of their age. It is conventional, in scientific writing, to give the author and date when referring to recent work. This is convenient for the reader who may want to know more about the statement, but it serves also the function of reiterating, by implication, that science consists of statements made by people about the conditions in which they witnessed certain events. It is impossible, however, to document the current basic assumptions in this way; they are taken for granted because enough competent people have held them long enough. Like the mores of a culture, they are anonymous and so all-pervasive as to be almost imperceptible. It requires an Einstein to offer any alternative.

Most of the time most of us are unconscious of the cultural factors that dominate our behaviour. It is only when a culture undergoes rapid change, as by the invention of a new technique, or when we have to come to terms with people of another culture, that we can begin to see that other ways of behaving are possible. In the same way we learn to speak our own language grammatically, without learning the rules of its grammar; but in learning another language it is easier to learn the rules than to habituate ourselves to the language by long apprenticeship. By learning the grammar of another language we may throw light on our own. Many of us first begin to understand the grammar of English which we have been unconsciously manipulating, when we have to learn French or Latin. Only by seeing how we resemble and differ from other people do we understand ourselves.

A world of one's own

A consequence of the selective nature of the receipt of information which was demonstrated in Chapters 2 and 3 is that we each live, within the same culture, even within the same family, in a world of our own. If my son and I go for half an hour's walk together we will give on our return a different account of what was in the street, he of the make, horse-power and date of the cars on the road, I of the range and prices of goods in shop windows. As a result of an apparently common experience, each of us will have added different information to his store, and as we have seen, those differences in the store of information will affect future receipts of information.

The analogy with feeding is a useful one, for neither in seeing nor in feeding is what is actually incorporated exactly the same as what is presented. Only part of the food taken into the mouth is digested, and the rest is rejected. That which is digested under-goes most complex changes before it enters the blood stream, and undergoes still further changes before it is assimilated into the fabric of the body or becomes useful as a source of energy.

A cow and a sheep feeding in the same meadow convert the grass into muscle and fat which, appearing in the butcher's shop or on the dinner plate, are to sight, taste and smell recognizably different—they are distinguishable as beef and mutton. Moreover different individuals of the same species transform their food into biologically distinguishable substances. While it is possible to graft the skin of one part of the body on to another part of the same individual it is not normally possible to exchange grafts between different individuals. The flesh of one person is biochemically different from that of every other. Members of a family sharing daily the same meals finger-print as it were, the substance they incorporate.

Although each person lives in his own world, only certain aspects of which he shares with other people, its building has been strongly affected by communication, mainly verbal, with other people which makes possible the testing of schemata.

Talking and testing

We have discussed how in learning to see, we build up schemata or assumptions by means of which incoming informa-tion is organized, and by acting on what we perceive these schemata are continually checked and modified. No such direct testing by physical manipulation of the outside world is possible for many of our schemata. Many of the schemata children have about the physical world for instance are of this kind; most children before the age of eight think that the sun and moon follow them when they go for a walk, and that their movement is controlled by the child's movement (Piaget, 1929). The majority of children of six years old believe that if a bridge breaks as a child is crossing a stream on the way home from having stolen some apples, it did so because of the child was naughty (Piaget, 1932). Remnants of childish ideas of retribution for wrong-doing linger on in the thinking of some adults about for instance, illness.

There is no check for such schemata other than talking about them, and thus comparing and contrasting them with other people's. Piaget's studies (1955) on the behaviour of children have demonstrated the importance of socialization in thinking. The early thinking of a child is egocentric; that is, the child does not trouble to make himself understood by others, to convince them or prove his point. The reasoning of the child is less deductive and less rigorous than that of the adult, because it is not concerned with proof or demonstration.

'Reality-adjusted thinking' (or 'reality-thinking') plays a larger and larger part as the child grows older. It has been defined as 'thinking specially adapted to the scientific purpose of enabling us to deal successfully with the objective world and its phenomena, by forming correct opinions about these phenomena, and about their causes and effects' (Crawshay-Williams, 1947). In adults 'autistic thinking' (or *autism*)—that is, thinking 'dominated by fantasy or by subjective trends, the material being uncorrected in its essential features by objective standards' (Warren, 1934)—occurs still in a more or less pure form in day-dreams and just before falling asleep or waking. Reality-adjusted thinking dominates a good deal of ordinary waking, conscious behaviour, but even here autistic behaviour is also often influential (McKellar, 1957).

To relate this to the terminology we have used we may say that the schemata of the child include many that have not yet been adequately tested, either directly, by using them in dealing with physical events or indirectly, or by comparing and contrasting them with other people's. Many of the schemata of the adult have been tested in these ways, but some remain untested because they have not been verbalized. Many of these are innocuous but others affect behaviour adversely; for instance, a person may fail to take effective action to avoid disease, or to get treatment for it, because his relevant schemata associate illness with justifiable or unavoidable punishment, as a child associates the breaking of a bridge with his own naughtiness.

Education and psychotherapy

One of the important effects of Freud's work was that we were forced to consider more seriously the possibility that a person's behaviour might be changed in a desirable direction by allowing him to talk, as distinct from talking to him or at him.

The mentally sick are those whose store of information is

inappropriately organized; their schemata or assumptions are such that the information they receive from the environment, both physical and social, does not lead to effective action. The trial-and-error methods by which, in the ordinary processes of living, schemata are continually modified in so-called normal or well-adjusted people seem to have failed. Many of these schemata were established early in life, and since, as we have seen in the 'Peasant Wedding' story, experiences become blurred and confused with each other with the passage of time, it is easy to see how responses to stimuli which evoke muddled schemata may be inappropriate. If a man sees a picture in terms of a story and cannot see which is which, why should he not see his boss as his father, and behave in consequence, perhaps inappropriately towards him?

Quite apart from the muddling effect of the passage of time, is the difficulty caused by the fact that many of the most potent schemata or assumptions were established before the child could talk, and having been made non-verbally, are very difficult to talk about; such schemata form part of the 'unconscious'. In specially devised situations however, the patient can be helped by the psychotherapist to explore even this part of his own store of information and to reorganize it where necessary.

While the psychotherapist is concerned mainly with helping the patient to verbalize and reorganize those schemata which are adversely influencing his behaviour, the teacher is traditionally concerned largely with passing on to the student the schemata that other people have found useful. The teacher's main job is to present new information in a suitably organized form and he is not much occupied with investigations as to how the new information he presents comes into relationships with the old schemata. The new schemata that are adopted may or may not modify the primitive schemata relating to the same subject; indeed sometimes the new schemata can be incorporated without modifying the old very much, and so can reinforce them even if they are not the kind that lead to effective action. For instance, the acceptance that smoking is causally related to cancer of the lung is compatible with the belief that smoking is reprehensible self-indulgence which is punished by disease.

Formal education is concerned largely with reality-adjusted

thinking, psychotherapy largely with autistic thinking as it inter-
feres with reality-adjusted thinking. The teaching method presently
to be described had characteristics of both traditional teaching
and psychotherapy.

The group as a testing ground

In the second part of this book I shall report on the treatment
of scientific problems by students in discussion groups. The
discussions were conducted in such a way that each student could
test his own schemata against those of his colleagues. In the
course of discussion some of the factors that had influenced the
judgment of each person, many of them unconsciously, became
apparent. Egocentric or autistic modes of thinking were seen to
be inextricably mixed with reality-adjusted thinking and the
autistic elements could be brought under conscious scrutiny, to
which they were not subject before.

The effectiveness of discussion in helping one to discover one's
unrecognized assumptions was described by a student thus:
'Later in the discussion I find how many angles there are of looking
at a problem which somehow do not occur to me. I tend to grasp
a few angles and am inclined to cling to them until a few moments
of heated discussion compel me to consider all the other many
angles' (Johnson, 1950).

Discussion in a group does for thinking what testing on real
objects does for seeing. We become aware of discrepancies
between different people's interpretations of the same stimulus
and are driven to weigh the evidence in favour of alternative
interpretations. Certain areas of one's private world are compared
and contrasted with other people's, and in seeing differences
between them it becomes possible to modify our own world if we
wish to. Instead of seeing our own mistakes by contrast with the
statements of an unquestioned authority as in the traditional
pupil-teacher relationship, we see a variety of interpretations of
the same stimulus pattern, and the usefulness of each must be
tested in its own right.

In attempting to arrange group discussion for this specific
purpose I have naturally been influenced by the experience of
many others who have worked with groups for different purposes.
Interest in the interaction of people in small groups has increased

enormously in the last two decades (see, for instance, Cartwright and Zander, 1953; Hare, Borgatta and Bales, 1955; Roseborough, 1953; Strodtbeck and Hare, 1954; Klein, 1956). For the present work, perhaps the most important observations are those concerning the effect of the behaviour of the leader on other members of the group and the establishing of different 'social climates' (e.g., see White and Lippitt, 1953; Bion, 1948–51).

More or less relevant to the project, also, are attempts to change the behaviour of people through group experiences, which have varied from those aimed at modifying very localized or specific types of behaviour (e.g., food habits; see Lewin, 1953) to the generalized changes of personality implied by psychotherapy. The latter includes a wide range of treatments of the group, e.g., the didactic group therapy of Klapman (1946), the psychodrama of Moreno (1945), analytic group therapy of Slavson (1950) and group-analysis of Foulkes (Foulkes and Anthony, 1957). The last has been particularly influential on this project. The 'free group discussion' which I shall describe in the second part of this book can be regarded as the 'free-floating discussion' of Foulkes adapted to serve the purpose of helping the members of the group to test those schemata that are relevant to certain scientific topics.

Part Two

EXPLORATIONS IN THINKING

This section examines what happens when students talk in such a way that they can discover and test the schemata they are using in dealing with scientific matters. It will be necessary first to outline the conditions of free group discussion in which this subject was studied.

5

The Nature of Free Group Discussion

THE essential difference between teaching in free group discussion and by ordinary didactic methods as in a lecture, is that the students talk to each other. In a lecture, the main lines of communication are between the speaker and the listeners (Fig. 11 (*a*)) and the students are not usually encouraged to talk to each other. In many cases of tutorial teaching in smaller groups the main channels of communication are still between the teacher and each student; the students may be encouraged to talk, to ask questions and answer them, but the main interchange is polarized towards the teacher (Fig. 11 (*b*)). In group discussion on the other hand, the emphasis is on the students talking to each other and the lines of communication form a network (Fig. 11 (*c*)).

In giving a lecture the teacher organizes the material in such a way that it will, he hopes, be comprehended, or assimilated, in roughly the way he intended it should be. Ideally, then, if he is successful all the students receive the same information, and it is the information he intended they should receive. In free group discussion, on the other hand, the students are presented with the same information (for example, two radiographs or an account of an experiment), but it soon becomes clear that they do not extract the same information from it, and learning depends on the fact that each extracts something different.

Discussion of the differences of their reactions involves discovering not only what factors influenced the kind of selection they made from the information presented, but it also involves exploring their own store of information. It is in emphasizing the important of individual differences in the store of information, in accepting the extremely subjective or personal nature of reaction to the stimulus pattern, that the discussion technique differs from the lecture technique.

The organization of the discussions is directed towards encouraging the students to talk freely and to listen to each other, and many environmental factors such as size of group and seating arrangements have complex effects on this.

Size of group

For administrative reasons it was convenient to have groups of twelve and although eight or nine persons is generally considered the optimum for many kinds of group work, in the particular circumstances the large number seemed to work fairly well. It was possible for one or two who wished to do so to remain

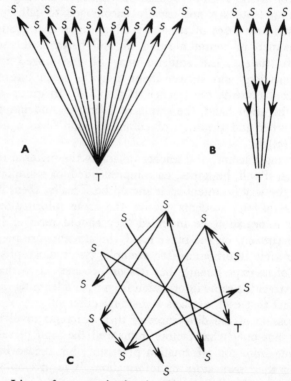

Fig. 11. Lines of communication in (A) a lecture, (B) a tutorial discussion, and (C) a group discussion. T, teacher; S, student

silent without social embarrassment. On the other hand students belonging to very active groups complained that they did not get a chance to talk enough.

The feelings students had about the size of the group were related to how they felt they ought to behave in the discussions, and their ideas about this underwent considerable modification. In the early part of the course, criticism was often expressed of those who talked too much, and those who felt they did not get a chance to talk complained that the group was too large. Later, when it became clear that a lot was to be learnt from listening, resentment turned against the silent ones who seemed to take advantage of what others said but made no contribution themselves.

Seating

It is essential for the students to face each other and the most convenient arrangement is for them to sit in a rough circle. The spatial arrangements have important interactions with behaviour. In my classes the students sat around a rectangular table, but there was not room for all of them and two or three seats would get pushed out of the main ring. These seats tended to be occupied by people who did not talk very much. It seemed that the shy or bored people tended to choose these seats and, having chosen them, found it more difficult to get a hearing if they did want to join in.

Sometimes peculiarities of seating position seemed to indicate what a student was feeling in relation to the others. For example, for the first two or three meetings one who had had experience of discussions on philosophy at school used to sit on the bench, above the others. He tried to organize the discussions along lines familiar to him until another member of the class explained that the idea was not to debate with well-prepared speeches, but just to talk spontaneously. Next week, the self-appointed chairman took his place with the rest on an ordinary chair. On another occasion, a student who had previously been a dominant member disagreed sharply with the rest of the group. At each clash of opinion he pushed his chair a little backward until he was quite outside the ring and then he became silent.

Special chairs or positions tend to acquire symbolic value and to be associated with fixed roles. Among the chairs there was one armchair, and because this was the one I ordinarily used at my writing-table it was more often than not at the end or head of the table. Students tended to avoid occupying this chair, as though preferring not to seem to usurp the teacher's place. I also tried to avoid it, and preferred to move around from week to week. In this way I hoped to dissociate myself as far as possible from the role of chairman, and also to encourage movement within the group, symbolizing flexibility of general behaviour.

Recording

During the last five years we recorded all discussions on tape. The effects of this on participants were doubtless very complex. Some students were probably inhibited but others were incited to talk the more. Many have said that they soon forgot the recording machines, as they became absorbed in the discussions. The recordings were of course invaluable for research, but they were also useful for teaching. Playing back an earlier part of a discussion, with comments, was often illuminating. It was also interesting for students to hear records of other groups, when they could see how the same problems arose but were differently handled. They could see how different modes of behaviour were possible and could change their own if necessary.

For example, a shy group was stimulated to much greater freedom of speech by listening to a rowdy group. By contrast, on one occasion a group was listening to another discussing classification. The main speaker was trying to explain how he felt there there must be an 'absolute' system of classification somewhere (see pp. 112-3) and he was having the greatest difficulty in expressing himself clearly—as someone said, 'you can hear him sweating with thinking'. The listeners were amused at his struggles and laughed uproariously. After some time, however, one of them said, 'But *they're* not laughing,' and they fell silent and began to listen as seriously as the recorded group had done.

Individual work

Before each discussion began, the students worked individually at an exercise which served as a basis for the discussion. This procedure came in for much criticism and the reason for it must be explained. The particular kind of group discussion envisaged was not intended to provide a group solution to a problem; the group was not a team in the sense that a specific job had to be done in co-operation. If this had been so a different approach would have been appropriate. (There is room for such techniques to serve other purposes in University teaching but that is another matter.) The aim was to provide a medium (the group discussion) in which each individual could learn about his own reactions. The intention was that each student should write down his own spontaneous reactions to a given stimulus (e.g., report of an experiment) in preparation for this.

My leaving the room while this work was being done was criticized on the grounds that time was wasted. It is very likely that if I had stayed more work would have been done in the sense that more words would have been written down, and attention would have been concentrated more specifically on the topic in hand. But against this must be balanced the other effects of the teacher's withdrawal. It acts as a demonstration that the responsibility for getting things clear rests with the individual; there are limits to what the teacher can do.

The criticisms expressed of this preliminary to discussion arose from the challenge it presented to accepted attitudes towards work and play. Students seemed to resent being asked to write, which they regarded as work, instead of being allowed to get straight down to talking, which they thought was easy and sometimes even fun. The exercise was regarded by some as a task, or a test imposed upon them; many of them wrote their names on the paper, or asked if they might write in pencil instead of in ink. Often students said that it was not fair to give them radiographs to compare, because some know more about them than others, as though they expected to be ranked according to their performance. Some resented the fact that very few people had the opportunity of presenting their script to the group and felt that their work had been wasted. They did not see the labour of writing as something that would help them personally, quite independently of whether it was marked by the teacher, or indeed seen by anybody else.

Sometimes strong feelings were aroused by the obligation to do the exercise. For example, one student wrote: 'I do enjoy the discussions, but they always leave me with the uncomfortable feeling that the sheet of paper I have written should not be left behind. I think the discussions will continue to be of use until I no longer have that guilty feeling.' This reaction is surprising in view of the conventional nature of the task; it is, after all, not unlike many of the pieces of homework or classwork they were expected to do as a matter of routine at school.

I have commented at length on these apparently trivial details of the arrangements in order to show the extreme complexity of the students' reactions. Besides subserving the main function intended more or less satisfactorily, any small feature of the arrangements had all sorts of side effects and subtle implications. Any event, however mundane it may seem, has symbolic meanings. In deciding on the most suitable arrangements one had to rely on judgment as to the balance of the good and bad effects. It was essential therefore to collect evidence continuously during the discussions as to what students were feeling in order to modify the proceedings if this were indicated. Such discussion of reactions also helped to clarify the general principles and encouraged the students to adjust themselves.

The behaviour of the students

As will become clear from the excerpts from tape recordings given on pages 94 and 112, the discussion is by formal standards rather chaotic. It is not usual for students to make long statements, indeed they are lucky if they are allowed to finish a sentence without being interrupted with expressions of agreement or contradiction, or by suggestions for modifications. The climate of the discussion may be illustrated by a remark made by a student who was very cross about this behaviour: 'You are the only polite one,' she said to me. 'You're the only one who stops talking when you're interrupted.'

In the early stages, as shown in the 'normal' discussion cited on pp. 94-97, it is usual for several students each to state their own view without considering very carefully how it compares or conflicts with others. This seems to follow naturally from their having worked individually on the exercise. Consequently, within the first twenty minutes or so, there will be thrown into the pool as it were, all the ideas that will be examined during the next hour. Different pieces of information are extracted from the same stimulus pattern by different students and interpreted as a result of selection from their own store of knowledge. During discussion each student witnesses the making of several other interpretations in addition to his own, and these pieces of information are added to his own store. The realization of how these selections came to be made, and the understanding of the new information, that is, linking it appropriately with his own relevant schemata, is a process of digestion.

This process takes time; when at the end of a discussion a recording of the first part was played back to the students they were often surprised to hear statements with which they now agreed, but which they had not taken in at the time. An example of this is the suggestion that 'commonly occurring' or 'most frequently found' could be substituted for 'average' in the passage under discussion. Among many other suggestions, this was usually made several times, sometimes by the same person, sometimes by more than one (see statements 13, 29–35, 68, pp. 95–97). But it was not until late in discussion that most of the group came to the opinion that this was a useful interpretation; often they felt that they had just invented it themselves, and were surprised to hear it occurring early in the discussion, apparently without effect. I say 'apparently without effect' advisedly, for it is my opinion that the same conclusion might not have been reached in the absence of these apparently ignored statements. For understanding the effectiveness of free group discussion in changing behaviour it is necessary to keep in mind the importance of the influence of background stimulation on behaviour (p. 56).

Expression of emotion

Another important difference between this method of teaching and the didactic lecture method is the extent to which emotion of various kinds is aroused and expressed. One gets the impression that many personal affinities and antipathies already established between students are brought into the discussion. These may be heightened by the discussions, since learning depends on seeing the similarities and differences in personal reactions. Serious disagreements may arise as indicated in the report of the evaluation of evidence discussion (p. 121) where there were clashes between opposing basic assumptions about human nature.

It is inevitable that some aspects of the course should be painful to some people, since it continually exposes the inadequacy of their customary approach to problems. A perspicacious student in an essay written two years after he had finished the course, said:

'My immediate interpretation of the first exercise (hand radiographs), despite having been informed that it was not such, was that it was some form of test with the result that I went into as much descriptive detail as possible and made many inferences which, as was pointed out to me later, could not be substantiated from the information on the X-ray alone. The impression derived from the discussion was not so much that one was not entitled to make these extraneous deductions but rather that the experiment was in some ways ridiculous for *I assumed that my own deductions would have been made, in any case, by any sensible radiologist*—so what was all the fuss about? Once this impression had established itself (of injured pride!) I realize now that I ignored the contemporaneous discussion and the implications behind the series of experiments were not even remotely realized until after two or three ensuing discussions, being effectively masked in my "rebuff".'

I do not think it is possible to protect students entirely from the discomfort of finding that they make mistakes. What is important is that they should recognize as this student clearly did, however late, to what extent their emotional reactions block learning. To find that many others have made the same mistake can be comforting, and is abundantly demonstrated, not only in the current discussion, but in the tape recordings of other groups.

Changing roles

It is clear that free group discussion involves different relationships between students and teacher from those appropriate to the usual teaching situation. It also involves different relations between the students themselves; sometimes the group works like a well-balanced orchestra, each playing a characteristic and it seems an almost pre-destined part. There is, for instance, the member who makes only four or five statements during one and a half hours, each a neat summary of the preceding conversation.

There are members who repeatedly bring the discussion back to what they regard as 'the point', others who as assiduously follow one red herring after another, and still others whose self-appointed task is to remind the group of what happened last week and the week before. The rate of contribution to discussion (that is, the number of interventions made) may remain fairly constant for any one person from week to week. But by contrast with these recognizably stable patterns there may be pronounced swings in both the amount and kind of contribution. One student who at the beginning talked a lot, and later became quiet, said when explaining the change:

'Well, at the beginning I regarded these as an excellent opportunity for discussing things. Later on we came to see that it is not so much that, but rather that you want to get something out of it, you tend then to take a different attitude to it, rather to want to know what others are thinking rather than to get your own view over and convince somebody else.'

A short account cannot hope to do justice to the variety of kinds of behaviour shown in free group discussions. Perhaps from the educational point of view the most important feature is the wide range of behaviour which is useful; in different ways it is as useful to listen as to talk; to agree as to disagree; to criticize as to approve. The topics covered are so varied that no one person can for long retain a dominant position as the most knowledgeable or the most clear-headed. Sooner or later even the cleverest finds himself in a web of confusion out of which he is helped may be by the most inarticulate. Often indeed it is the academically weak student who can offer a direct common-sense way out of the maze in which they all are stuck. Any one student may be at one moment the teacher, at another the pupil, and the tact, patience and skill which students severally or jointly may command when they undertake to teach another are worth seeing.

The behaviour of the teacher

The teacher takes the role of listener instead of main speaker in free group discussions. Long speeches are inappropriate, whether made by teacher or students, and fortunately at these close quarters, there is less protection than in the lecture theatre against restive movements or the glazing of eyes. It is the timing of contributions that is most important; the same statement made at different points in the discussion may have quite different effects.

My main task was to make it possible for students to compare and contrast the statements they made with those that others made. The first thing then was to encourage spontaneity of speech, which was done mainly by listening and giving signs of having heard—hard discipline for one used to lecturing. I tried to be socially reassuring and avoided making statements which could seem to reprove any individual, or even to praise, because praise of one implies by contrast criticism of the others. Sladen (1956), describing the training of huskies for work in the Antarctic, said, 'One should not give individual attention to one particular dog when trying to cultivate team spirit. For instance, if you pat one dog you should go round and pat them all.' The students were much harsher to each other than I was to them. I tried to use neutral language and to direct emotion into effective channels, so that they could be usefully anxious about the difficulties of thinking clearly and not be diverted by being anxious about its becoming apparent that they had difficulties in thinking clearly.

On the whole I avoided also explicitly correcting mistakes (again hard discipline for a teacher) unless they were very dangerous ones. Usually statements were challenged by other participants so promptly that it was not necessary for me to do anything. (A student wrote, 'One has to consider one's words most carefully before giving utterance, or some ten outraged fellow-students are likely to tear one's opinion to shreds.') When I felt intervention was called for I avoided expressing my own opinion and tried to direct their attention to anomalies and inconsistencies in what they had said, leaving them free to find a better formulation themselves. This behaviour on the part of the teacher is often frustrating. The students tended to want answers to such questions as, 'What ought we to have said?' and 'What are we expected to do?' If these questions are answered directly, they do not easily distinguish between what is true because an authority, the teacher, has said so and what is true in the sense that it can be verified by other tests that they make themselves.

Sometimes the difficulties of thinking and expressing themselves clearly were so great that they got frustrated and angry. This happened almost invariably in the discussion on 'normal'. Well-intentioned efforts on my part to clarify the situation even with the most carefully designed statements were remarkably ineffective. One or two might listen as though they understood what I said, but most were quiet only to save their breath and rushed back into their own confusions as soon as they could without being obviously rude. It seemed as though the associations that each person had to the word were extensive and tangled; the teacher could make it possible for the student to recognize that there was a muddle, but could not do much to help to tidy up. That a long struggle is necessary to do this is indicated by the fact that students went on discussing the subject long afterwards.

There are very serious limitations on the extent to which a teacher can help a student to think as distinct from giving him part of an established body of knowledge. Two aspects of the work of the teacher are important however; these are helping to make the pattern of the course apparent, and facilitating the transfer of training.

Chaos and pattern

It will be clear that freedom and spontaneity of discussion is essential to this type of course, and that this entails the danger that it may appear chaotic and meaningless. It often seems that discussion goes off the point, but it must be remembered that what is a red herring to one person is relevant to another. It can be taken for granted that a completely irrelevant topic could not arise; often one or more sudents may show intense interest in an apparently irrelevant remark, either by insisting on developing it further, even at the cost of boring the rest, or by recalling it in other contexts. It often happened that a student spontaneously announced that the relevance of certain passages which bored or puzzled him at the time had become clear in retrospect, or on listening to recordings. It is the teacher's job to make clear the relation of such significant red herrings to the main topic.

It is also important to show the relationship of one discussion to previous ones, to show how the same principles of selection and interpretation hold throughout for receipt of information through any channel. The pattern of the discussions is, however, a bit like the Hidden Man; some people seem to see it easily and some not at all during the course, though there is evidence that it may become clear some time after. Others see bits of pattern that most of us do not, as some see in the same picture little men in one corner or another, in right or left profile, with large or small noses, upside-down or on their side, but not the man we would like them to see.

This seeing initially a different pattern from the one intended is all right if it is corrected early enough, as it was by the student quoted above (p. 74). On the other hand a student who was very pleased at first because he seemed to expect that some magic recipe for clear thinking would be given, nursed his disappointment through the whole course and seemed to learn little.

There is a danger in the teacher summarizing discussion in too final a way, because it tends to inhibit further thinking by the students. They should not be given the impression that decisions can be made tidily and finally on the matters discussed in the course, but rather that the function of the discussion is to start them thinking. Again judgment is necessary to decide where the balance should be held between the demands for a feeling of security, with the risk of inflexibility, on the one hand, and the need to keep potentialities for further growth with possible anxiety, on the other.

Transfer of training

The other important task for the teacher is to encourage transfer of training. There is reason to believe that training acquired in one field is not necessarily automatically transferred to another, but that the transfer is facilitated if the subject can see the relevance of the new field to the one in which the training took place (Burt, 1947). I made a point therefore of trying to relate continuously what was happening in the discussions both to everyday life and to the job of being a student and prospective doctor. In this way it was hoped to prevent the discussions remaining of purely academic or theoretical interest and to make them of practical use in the sense that they would change behaviour in the work field in the desired direction.

The nature of the teacher's contribution

I am well aware that readers who are unfamiliar with group discussions may find this description of the behaviour of the participants—and especially, perhaps, that of the teacher—somewhat inadequate. I have, therefore, attempted to summarize below my way of thinking about behaviour in free group discussions, in order to make clear what has determined the kind of contribution I tried to make.

The aim in scientific work is to extract information of predictive value from a given stimulus pattern. The information that each individual acquires from a stimulus pattern depends on how it fits into his pre-existing store of information, that is, what schemata or assumptions come into operation. The schemata interact with each other sometimes freely, sometimes more rigidly. The likelihood of obtaining information of good predictive value is increased if the schemata are flexibly related to each other, so that various combinations can be scanned and their usefulness tested by reference to the stimulus pattern.

In free group discussion, those parts of each individual's store of information which are for him relevant to the scientific topic under consideration, and which help or hinder him to get information of predictive value, become clear. What a student says he sees in, for instance, hand radiographs, depends on the way his schemata of recently received, specialized information about techniques of radiography are related to older, more generalized, schemata of the kind that 'things which are alike in some respects are alike in others'. The recently received information is easily verbalized; much of it has been received verbally. The older schemata are far less easily verbalized; they may have been made and reinforced largely through non-verbal channels. The student is usually not aware that he is using them, but their existence can be inferred from verbal and other behaviour. Because the student is not aware of them he does not question the validity of using them on a particular occasion, and therefore often uses them inappropriately and fails to extract information of predictive value. Learning in free group discussion is a process of identifying, through verbalization, the associations between schemata, so that the new information can be dissociated from those schemata with which it is automatically associated, and can be seen to be potentially relevant to many schemata, instead of to a few only.

By studying the reactions of many groups of students to the same scientific topic it was possible to identify and describe recurring patterns of behaviour or modes of employing schemata. Reference to these was made at appropriate points during sub-sequent discussions to help to clarify and broaden the students' understanding of their own ways of behaving. From the reactions of the students to my remarks some clues could be gained as to whether the guesses I made about the nature of the association of schemata were useful ones. The project thus involved a cyclical process in which it is hardly useful to consider research and teaching as distinct activities.

I hope that I have not made the task of the conductor of free group discussion seem too onerous in my attempt to make clear that it demands activity quite different from that required by didactic teaching. Much of the work ordinarily done by the teacher in tutorials—questioning, criticizing, asking for evidence, controlling the too vocal or encouraging speech in the silent—is taken over sooner or later in various ways by members of the group. This acceptance of responsibility is itself a maturing process which must be encouraged, and perhaps the teacher can best assist by having faith that it will occur.

Free group discussion in education

Before closing this chapter on the nature of free group dis-cussion I would like to attempt to forestall certain misunder-standings that might otherwise arise. For many people, the schemata which come into operation in reaction to the stimulus pattern of 'group', are such that the material I have presented may not be interpreted in the way I intended. The word 'group' has so many connotations of 'mass', 'herd', 'crowd', 'clique', 'team', that it is easy to think that any form of organized group behaviour involves the subjugation of the individual. Further, the term 'brainwashing' which implies removing one dogma in order to make room for another may spread its unfavourable aura over any reference to an introspective kind of group discussion; and those who have studied the processes that occur in groups are felt to have some dark power that enables them to manipulate people more easily in groups than singly, and to ends which the rest of us consider undesirable. I would repeat, therefore, that the aim of the course of free group discussions described here was to help the individual participants to reach a better understanding of some of the factors that affect scientific judgment, in order to secure better control over them, so that they can make sounder judgments. The aim was to provide in the group a medium in which the individual learned ways of behaving which would be useful to him when the group had dissolved.

As to what other fields of education could be favourably influenced by free group discussion techniques, to what extent they might usefully replace or supplement traditional didactic instruction in specified fields, this question can only be answered by experiment. The new problems that the Second World War threw up, of instructing adults to whom lectures and conventional class-room methods were unacceptable or ineffective, have already stimulated the development of various discussion techniques in adult education. They are also used here and there in industry and commerce in ways more and less sophisticated, to stimulate problem-solving activities and 'creative' or 'productive' thinking.

It is possible, however, that suitably adapted they might be most useful where at present least used, where autistic thinking is most dominant, namely in teaching children. Our methods of formal education are still governed by a notion that children's little heads are empty, or at least emptier than they should be, whereas the truth is that it is because they are too full of what we do not understand that they are difficult to teach. And if the trouble is that far from being unreceptive to our lessons they became too docile, unimaginative or stereotyped in their thinking, we should keep in mind that the teaching situation uses and may reinforce the authority-dependency relationship; even a non-authoritarian and child-orientated adult is bigger, heavier and more powerful than the child to whom he orientates. Reality-adjusted thinking is transmitted largely through adults and tends to become associated with authority; we do not know what the effects would be of loosening the association at an early stage, by arranging conditions in which children can interact intellectually more freely than is common at present.

But whatever their value in this or other fields of instruction may turn out to be, it may legitimately be stressed that in free group discussion techniques there lies a promising tool for investigating those hidden processes of our own and other people's thinking which so powerfully govern our behaviour, and about which we know so little. In the following chapters a report will be given of some of the processes, as they are seen in free group discussion, which are involved in the thinking of medical students about certain scientific topics.

6

Seeing and Thinking

IN the next four chapters I shall examine in turn the topics on which the discussion course was based. It was natural to begin the course with a study of the problem of observing since biologists spend much of their time getting information visually from organisms or parts of organisms. To be able to observe accurately and comprehensively, and to draw reasonable conclusions from the observations is an important skill in biology. It is a skill which is not easy to learn.

Students know how difficult it is to look with any profit at, say, a skull, or down the microscope at a section of skin, until they have had some kind of instruction in what to look for and preferably have a diagram beside them. Teachers know that if students have such aids to observation they commonly exhibit the Three Triangles reaction; they tend to see what they expect to see whether it is there or not. Many a student's drawing resembles a textbook figure more than the specimen in front of him; and the more complicated the specimen is and the more unfamiliar, the more its picture looks like the book. How to tell students what to look for without telling them what to see is the dilemma of teaching. In the terms used in the previous chapters, the problem is how to help them to organize their store of information in flexible schemata so that new information can be taken in and appropriately assimilated.

This chapter is called 'Seeing and Thinking' because although it is common to believe that in scientific work one first makes observations and then draws conclusions from them, the two activities are in practice inextricably mixed. In common English the distinction is often blurred; 'to see' is used figuratively to mean understand, or consider, or imagine, or inquire. To see in

the nonfigurative sense implies that information is received from
the outside world through the eyes; while in the figurative sense
we can see with our eyes shut in the dark. In discussing the Two
Shapes, the Three Triangles or the Hidden Man you will soon
find the words 'see' and 'think' being used almost interchangeably.
You will find it difficult to distinguish between what you saw and
what you thought you saw.

I shall now examine in some detail what happens when
medical students look at radiographs, in order to illustrate further
the interrelation of seeing and thinking. By seeing I refer to the
receiving of information through the eyes, and by thinking I refer
to the processes of rearranging information already received.

Seeing differences

We are always making use of our ability to compare and
contrast things. When we choose an apple from a plateful we
have very rapidly compared and contrasted it not only with the
others we reject, but also with our schemata of various kinds of
apples we have known, from which we have learnt roughly what
sort of taste and texture apples of a given appearance are likely to
have. In the same way a doctor examining a patient is comparing
and contrasting him with what he thinks ought to be the man's
condition in health, and with other patients he has known whose
illnesses might be the same.

I shall attempt to illustrate the complexities of this kind of
behaviour by reference to what medical students say when they
are shown two radiographs (Plate VII) and given the task:
'List the differences you can see between the two hands.' The
account is based on experience of forty-two discussions covering
a period of seven years. About twelve students took part in a
discussion, and each lasted about one and a half hours. Although
the groups differed very much according to the varied personalities
of the members, the same topics came up repeatedly, so that the
ways of behaving reported here can be regarded as common in
this kind of student in this type of situation.

Descriptions and inferences

Before discussing what the students, who have considerable
biological knowledge, said about the radiographs, it is perhaps

worth noting what other people agree can be seen in them. This is given on page 86. To avoid tiresome circumlocution, we have referred to shadows of flesh and bone rather than to grey or white patches although this involves making inferences from biological knowledge. With this qualification, however much or however little you know about hands and photographs and radiographs, you will be able to check for yourself the validity of the statements made there. They concern differences in size, number, shape and distribution of the shadows in the prints, that is, statements which can be investigated by reference to the prints alone. Such descriptive statements (sometimes called 'facts' or 'data') have a high likelihood of being correct, that is, they will usually be confirmed by other observers.

The students, however, do not on the whole make such bare precise statements, but tend instead to make such statements as, 'A is a young hand and B an old hand', 'the bones in B have fused', 'A is a live hand, B is a skeleton'. In making this kind of statement (an inference or conclusion) they are going beyond the information given, combining parts of their own store of common and biological knowledge with the information presented by the picture. The truth of such statements cannot be investigated by reference to the prints alone because they are made about the students' schemata, as well as about the image on their retina. Compared with descriptive statements inferences have a lower likelihood of being correct.

As we know well, people do not agree so readily on conclusions as they do on facts, but any reader who has struggled through the list of facts or descriptive statements on page 86 will concede that conclusions or inferences are more interesting and useful; they are what we act upon. In medicine and science it is important to keep clear about this difference between the validities of descriptions and inferences, for it is very easy to think you are making a descriptive statement when you are making an inference, as we shall see in what follows.

The various members of the discussion group submitted different lists. In discussing them we began to discover some of the factors that had influenced what kind of information different people had derived from the pictures.

When the statement that A is a young hand, B an old hand

Description of the hand-radiographs (Plate VII)

A and B are tracings of the outlines of the white shadows (bones) seen in the X-ray images on the photograph. The comparable rays of bone shadows (fingers and palm) on each tracing have been numbered in roman figures I–V inclusive. The bone outlines on tracing A have been numbered 1–28. The bone shadows on tracing A judged to correspond in relative position with those on tracing B have been given the same numbers.

The following differences can be seen:—

1. The corresponding bone shadows are smaller in A than in B.
2. The bone outlines labelled 1'–15' and 27' and 28' in A are not present in B.
3. The spaces between the bone outlines are larger in most cases in A than in B. In B these spaces are entirely absent in some regions, the bone outlines overlapping.
4. The bone shadows in the wrist region of A are discrete from each other (with the exception of 22 and 23). There are ten shadows (or nine if 22 and 23 are one). They are simple in shape and homogeneous in whiteness. In B they are close together, angular and heterogeneous in whiteness. It is difficult to trace the outlines in B with certainty; there might be only six.
5. A diffuse shadow (flesh) between the bone shadows is clearly visible in A, but scarcely visible in B.
6. There are many differences in the shape of the outlines of the long bones 1–19, and 27, 28, especially at their approximating surfaces.

Explanation

The pictures were made from radiographs of the hand of a normal child $7\frac{1}{2}$ years old (A) and a normal adult (B).

The identification of the separate bone outlines in A with those in B, particularly in the wrist region, is only possible by interpreting the shadows on the assumption that the pictures represent two normal human hands at different stages of growth.

In the child there are seven wrist bones (shadows 20–26), the other three shadows in the wrist region being epiphyses of long bones (15' is the epiphysis of 15, the metacarpal of the thumb; 27' that of 27, the ulna, and 28' that of 28, the radius). In the adult these epiphyses have fused with their long bones, so that the equivalents of 15', 27' and 28' of A are not seen as separate shadows in B.

In the adult wrist there are eight bones, an extra centre of ossification having appeared; this bone, not present in the child, overlaps 26 in B, causing the dense shadow. The dense shadow below the thumb in B is also due to the overlapping of two separate bones, equivalent to 22 and 23 of A. (The dense white patch on 20 in B is due to a projection of the bone itself).

The explanation makes it clear that the pictures are difficult to interpret and we did not expect students to be able to do this. We did not expect them even to know what the limits of the wrist are, that for instance in A 27' and 28' belong to the arm region, and 15' to the palm. In fact they usually recognized that 27' and 28' are the epiphyses of the ulna and radius respectively, but regarded 15' as a wrist bone instead of the epiphysis of the metacarpal of the thumb.

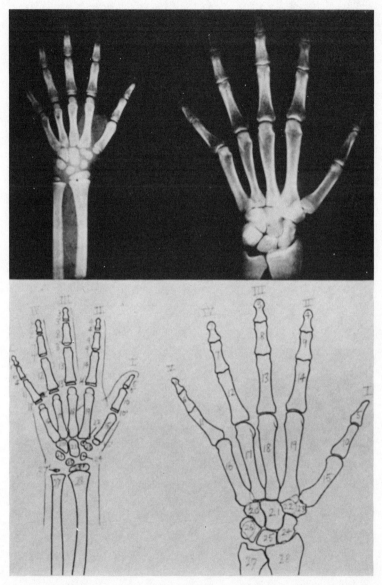

PLATE VII. List the differences you can see between the two hands
(*See facing page*)

was discussed, it appeared that it was made because of the smaller size of A, and the greater number of bones in it. In discussing size it soon became clear that many students had taken for granted that the size of the prints was a sure guide to the relative sizes of the hands themselves. In support of this, they said the hands must have been radiographed side by side on the same plate because there was no dividing line visible. However, others who were more familiar with radiography and photography pointed out that this was not necessarily so. Many things could have been done to the prints; one was not justified in assuming that they were reduced to the same scale, and one could not therefore safely say anything about the relative ages of the hands on the basis of the size of the prints. Thus, a statement that one student had regarded as a 'fact', i.e., undeniably true, another regarded as an 'inference' or 'conclusion'. To quote a student on this point: 'It was surprising to hear what others read out as observations without realizing what assumptions they had made, and most disconcerting when one fell into the trap oneself' (Johnson, 1950).

In discussing the second point, which was held to support the view that A was a younger hand than B, that is, the difference in number of bones, most students felt sure that the smaller number of bones in B had resulted from fusion of certain bones, which were separate in A. For instance, they said that certain long bones had fused with their epiphyses, e.g., 10 with 10; (this does happen in normal development). Many also thought that the small bones in the wrist region of A had fused together in various ways to form the smaller number in B (this does not happen in normal development). While most agreed in principle they argued over which bones fuse with which. They disagreed so much over the details that they began to doubt whether they could with certainty match up the bones in the two hands, and sooner or later someone said that perhaps there were more bones in the wrist of B than appeared; the outlines were vague and in parts the shadows were so dense that it was possible that bones overlapped each other. What is interesting is that the idea of fusion was so dominating that other possible explanations for the difference in the apparent number of bones were overlooked— for instance the possibility that in B bones overlapped each other, or that some bones had been resorbed during development.

In some cases students who actually knew previously that there are eight bones in the adult wrist 'forgot' it in their attempt to use the hypothesis of fusion to explain why only six bones were visible. This is a very clear example of selecting from the store of knowledge.

Here we have also an example of selection from the information presented. As in the case of the Three Triangles, the postman, or the button on the vest, a conclusion about 'meaning' had limited the perception of the observers, causing them to ignore information which did not fit the ordained pattern, the chosen schema. In this case, people who said there were six wrist bones in B were not making use of two pieces of information in the picture: that in B the shadows are so irregular in shape and close together that one cannot distinguish and count the bones they represent; and that in parts the shadows are much denser than in others, and the bones may be more than one layer thick. We shall return later to the importance of keeping alternative hypotheses in mind as a way of extracting the maximum possible valid information from a radiograph.

Further consideration of the statement that the bones had fused in B shows that it was an attempt to read into the pictures something about the history of B and the future of A. It was an attempt to explain B in terms of A, to relate them together. It was based on the presupposition that B had passed through a stage represented by A. This implied that the pictures were taken from the same species. The students were predisposed to think that this was the case, because as medical students they were naturally primarily interested in the human and the word 'hand' (not 'paw' or 'forelimb') tends to imply the human, though it may not be restricted to it. When they discussed the matter, but not until, they realized that they did not know enough about fore-limbs to be sure that they were both human hands; one or both might be that of a monkey, or even an amphibian or reptile, for all they knew. This underlines the importance of the formulation of instructions as one of the factors which determines observation and remind us of the Ambiguous Figures. If the instruction had been 'List the differences you can see between the two pictures', the students' reaction to the same stimulus pattern might have been different in many respects.

To summarize; during the discussion it became clear that the apparently simple 'factual' statement that 'B is an older hand than A' is an inference which had been arrived at as a result of picking up a number of clues, calling on past experience and information which was more or less relevant, ignoring the limitations of their knowledge, and inadequately testing hypotheses to estimate the probability of their being correct. The inferences the students had made were not arrived at as a result of a series of logical steps, but swiftly and almost unconsciously. The validity of the inferences was usually not inquired into, indeed the process was usually accompanied by a feeling of certainty of being right, and consequently the discussion of incompatible views sometimes be came very heated. Frequently the correct inference had been made (as with the statement that A was a younger hand than B), and then dis cussion did not change the formulation of the end result, but only brought to light the processes involved in getting it.

We can now attempt to relate the behaviour of students in this situation to the more general statements previously made about perception. It is evident that selection occurred both from the information presented and from the store of information. The factors that influenced this selection ranged from easily modifiable ones to deep-seated, personal ones. Consider the statement that 'hand A is younger than hand B because it is smaller'. A feature of the context which influences the making of this statement was that the two pictures were on the same piece of paper and there was no obvious line between them. It was thus easy to assume that the radiographs had been prepared from hands lying side by side, and therefore that the pictures must be to the same scale. This clue could be removed by cutting the paper between the two hands. There were also deeper or personal factors concerning general attitude which cannot be so easily modified. Some people took it for granted that any sensible teacher would not give students pictures of different scale to compare, while others were by nature suspicious, and looking for tricks or catches in everything, assumed that the pictures might not be of the same scale.

Of overriding importance in determining the kind of statement made about the radiographs was the 'effort after meaning' to use Bartlett's phrase (Bartlett, 1932); the tendency to try to extract as much meaning as possible from the pictures—or to put as much into them. The students were not satisfied with bare statements of the 'facts' but tried to find relationships between the pictures, and to explain the origin of some of the appearances. There were among the students some who claimed that they deliberately adopted a 'scientific' attitude, but even if they said that they were making a list of facts and not of conclusions or inferences, they often found themselves drawing inferences. For instance a man who said he recognized that two approaches were possible and had decided to list only facts, nevertheless talked about 'unfused pieces' in A (instead of using non-committal language such as 'separate'), implying that they could or would later fuse as he thought they had done in B.

The point of the discussion was not, of course, only to show that mistakes were made, but to show that the mistakes were of specific kinds, not random, and were determined by ways of behaving which serve us well in most cases. It is not irrefutable 'facts' that we find interesting, and that we act on, but the inferences we make from them, often without recognizing the limits of their validity, without questioning how safe they are.

Observer error

Mistakes in the conclusions people make when looking at things are unfortunately not confined to students and attention has recently been drawn to the phenomenon of observer error in medicine (Lancet, 1954, 1955; Johnson, 1955). One of the most striking demonstrations of this arose out of an inquiry into the most suitable radiographic technique for making routine chest examinations (Birkelo *et al.*, 1947). Five chest experts examined 1,256 radiographs and classified each as positive or negative for tuberculosis. There were considerable discrepancies between the experts' opinions, for instance one expert picked out fifty-six positives and another one hundred. When the experts reassessed the same films two months later there were discrepancies between the first and second opinions; thus one reader picked out fifty-nine films as positive in his first reading and seventy-eight in the second. Of his first reading positives 7 per cent were returned negative on second reading, and 29 per cent of his second reading positives had been returned negative on first reading.

There is now a great deal of evidence that such discrepancies are found whenever they are looked for, as when experts assess the progress of disease by examining a series of radiographs from the same patient. 'In judging a pair of films for evidence of progression, regression or stability of disease in patients with pulmonary tuberculosis, two readers are likely to disagree with each other in almost one-third of the cases and a single reader is likely to contradict himself in approximately one-fifth of the cases.' (Yerushalmy *et al.*, 1951.)

Even the reading of instruments is subject to observer error. In reading a burette, for instance (Renbourn and Ellison, 1950), a preference for certain digits rather than others may be shown, the preference varying with the individual and with time. There is also a marked tendency for a worker to obtain an 'expected result'. Of particular interest to us, is the suggestion made by the authors of this paper that the error is probably due to parallax, the observer unconsciously moving his head to a position which gives the desired result. If this is so, we have an example of bodily movements being made to ensure that the information received will fit a schema, and this done unconsciously. This may be generally the case; with for instance, the Hidden Man and the Three Triangles, the scanning movements of the eyes when interpretation A is being made may be different from those used when interpretation B is being made. Just as the building up of schemata about the size and shape of playing-cards for example, is done with information received as a result of picking up the cards, as well as of looking at them, it may be that the fitting of new visual information into old schemata is done with the co-operation of muscular movements; not only the brain, but other parts of the body may be at work even if we seem to be sitting quite still, just looking and thinking.

The phenomenon of observer error among experts is not cited to spread alarm about the inadequacy of medical skill. In practise, the treatment of a patient seldom depends on the results of a single test. But its widespread occurrence indicates the need to investigate those factors that affect the judgment of experts, in order to discover the conditions in which judgments of greater predictive value can be made.

The demonstration that even experts make mistakes was a

source of comfort to the students, not merely because they had glimpsed the feet of clay and could gloat over, rather than quail before, authority; it showed that the tiresome kind of errors in observation for which students get reprimanded are not easily dismissable as due to youth, ignorance, carelessness or wilful stupidity, nor will the passage of time, increased experience or strengthening of moral fibre put an end to them. Observation in science, whether during training, or in the practice of the most exquisitely developed skill, involves guessing, just as seeing in ordinary life does (and I use the word 'guessing' here to emphasize the precarious nature of the act, which the expression 'making a judgment' elides). What we are concerned with is learning to make the guess as good as possible.

7

Using Words

WE have seen that in receiving information visually we are influenced by the immediate context, and by our personal disposition. The same is true for receipt of information verbally.

I shall attempt to illustrate this by reference to what students said regarding their understanding of the words 'normal' and 'average'. They were given a short paragraph from a book on anatomy containing the terms 'average body', 'average condition', 'anatomical normal type' and 'the "normal" in Anatomy and Physiology'. They were asked to write what they thought the author meant by these terms, and also to give all the definitions of 'normal' they could think of.

At the beginning of the discussions the students usually agreed that the meaning of the passage was clear, but they soon disagreed when they tried to define more precisely what they thought the author meant. They found that each was talking about what *he* meant by average and normal, and this was not the same as what the others meant. In some cases a student thought that the word 'average' has only one well-defined meaning, e.g., the arithmetical mean, or pertaining to it. More often, students recognized that 'average' has several meanings (e.g., common, usual, ordinary, like the majority), but felt that only one meaning was 'permissible' in this context. It was impossible, however, to secure agreement on words that could be satisfactorily substituted for 'average', because different students had different ideas about what was the 'permissible' meaning in this particular passage.

A particular confusion about 'average' which frequently occurred is of special interest to scientists, because of the technical use of the word. In order to clarify what students understand by 'average', I asked them how they would find the average height of men aged eighteen in England. It was surprisingly common for some to suggest that the heights of the very tall and the very short men should be eliminated from the calculation, and the arithmetical mean taken of the rest, the 'normal'. Needless to say there was great difficulty in deciding where the line should be drawn, and there was resistance to accepting the fact that even if a satisfactory division were agreed the resulting figure would relate to only part of the population.

What 'the average body' means

The difficulties of thinking clearly when using such words as 'normal' and 'average' will be illustrated by an extract from the tape recording of part of a discussion about the average body. The reader may find this transcript tedious to follow, and to those used to logical argument it will seem hopelessly chaotic. It is given here to illustrate some general characteristics of the early part of a discussion as well as to indicate the difficulties the students had, in this particular discussion, with the word 'average'.

There were eleven students in the group and the voices of six can be recognized; they are numbered in the order in which they spoke. Statements whose authors could not be identified are attributed to 'X'. The students had begun by discussing what the author meant by 'average body', and this extract started two minutes later. The passage quoted here lasted 4 minutes 5 seconds. The statements have been numbered consecutively so that we can refer to them later.

1	Student 1	He's using average in a loose sort of sense. I think you're more likely to come across. . . .
2	2	I think it's used in the way you talk about the man in the street.
3	(Several)	Yes, mmm.
4	2	And there's no such thing as the man in the street.
5	(Several)	No.
6	X	I don't think so.
7	3	I think he means by it, the man in the street is the anatomically normal type.
8	X	Yes.

9	(Great hubbub)	No, No.
10	1	I think the average body means the average sort of thing you come across. If it's really out of the normal it isn't what you would call average, because it's a sort of guide to the thing you normally——
11	4	Oh, I say it's a guide to the body, to a body——.
12	1	—— thing you usually get.
13	4	—— where you find, the parts of which would be those which you most commonly find.
14	3	No, that's the normal type.
15	1	That's the normal type. That's a collection of things you see.
16	5	The average body is one that can vary from the normal type in slight——.
17	X	Very slight.
18	5	——ways but no distinct variation, no big variation.
19	1	That's what I mean by using average loosely.
20	2	——just because we can't define this strange thing and we use it just as a pointer to a vague . . . it's like pointing to a middle of a group, and just saying something in there. Because we can't define what the average man is, or the man in the street, or the average anything we use that sort of vague term.
21	5	No, I think perhaps, mmm——.
22	(Several mumblings of dissent)	
23	1	That would be more the anatomical normal type.
24	X	Yes.
25	3	Surely you can just sum it up by saying it's the type most frequently met with.
26	(Several)	No.
27	X	No, that's the——.
28	X	I disagree.
29	4	I disagree. The type most frequently met is the average.
30	X	Yes, it is the average.
31	4	The average . . . is the one most commonly found.

		If you draw a graph and you get a nice big peak in the middle you say that is the average.
32	X	Ah, yes.
33	4	Well if you draw a graph of all the occurrences of all the different wiggles in a certain artery or vein, you go through a few thousand and then you get a nice big bump in the middle of the graph which conforms to that most commonly found.
34	X	Yes.
35	4	*That* is the average.
36	(Several shouting)	No.
37	X	Normal.
38	2	Is it the average body?
39	X	That's the normal.
40	3	No, I think he means by that the average condition.
41	X	The average——.
42	3	The average condition, but not the average body.
43	X	I don't.
44	X	Well a body——.
45	6	You can't talk about averages, when you're, when you're considering two extremes really. For instance you can't say that average people are black or white, and you certainly couldn't say they were grey, could you? Which would you say the average person is? you can't talk about the average when you consider the whole human race, ——.
46	X	You can.
47	6	——only when you, only when you consider a narrow selection that doesn't vary greatly.
48	4	If you consider the whites you can say which is the most white of the whites——.
49	6	Exactly but you can't consider them both together.
50	4	——and which is the least white of the whites.
51	2	Don't you think that there are so many things which can vary in a body that it, that one generally talks about the average of one thing?
52	4	That's why I said parts in my definition.
53	2	Well, he's talking about the average *body*.
54	1	I think he meant by the average body the body we meet with.
55	X	Yes.

56	1	*Any* body we meet with.
57	5	Yes, definitely.
58	3	Which doesn't show very gross variations, as a double head. In other words the sort of thing we're liable to find on the dissecting table. That's what he meant by it.
59	X	You mustn't——.
60	3	I don't think he was correct in meaning that——.
61	5	You mustn't . . . too much about this average, because in this sense it isn't being used as a mathematical average.
62	3	No, it's not being used as a mathematical average.
63	X	You can't use it.
64	3	That's why I disagree with Mr. 4, he's trying to . . . make the author mean what the author didn't. You were using average loosely and not mathematically, and we were asked what the author means by the word or what he should mean by the word.
65	2	Well, he certainly means something.
66	3	And then later on he uses the term average condition in a mathematical sense.
67	X	Mmm.
68	3	And not the everyday sense. The average condition being the one most frequently found.
69	5	Yes, and not the mathematical average.
70	X	No.
71	4	Well, that is the mathematical average.

At this early stage in the discussion it seems that each person was trying to express his own idea of the word 'average', that is, was exploring his own store of information rather than receiving anything new. It is probable that this mode of behaviour is partly determined by the preceding individual work. A student sometimes repeated the same idea several times (for example, Student 1, statements 1, 10, 54, 56). Agreement and disagreement with other people's statements were freely expressed but not apparently with much careful consideration of their implications. Notice that although they were supposed to be discussing 'average body' they did not restrict their attention to this, but were concerned simultaneously with other terms used in the quotation they had studied, such as 'normal type'.

The discussion often became very heated. Many students found it the most interesting of the course (and some the most tedious), and often they continued to talk about the word 'normal' for hours afterwards over coffee or in the dissecting room. Before attempting any further description of the progress of discussion, we will pause a moment to see how the students dealt with the second part of the exercise, 'give all the definitions of "normal" you can think of' when each was coolly working individually before the battle began.

Definitions of 'normal'

Three scripts from members of the same group are quoted entire to indicate how the matter was handled by different individuals. The range of variation is surprising in view of the fact that I left the room while this exercise was being done, and the students could talk to each other if they wanted to. The number in brackets shows the area of meaning to which the statement was subsequently allocated, as will be explained below.

Script A
Of sound mind (3)
Perpendicular (5)
Containing the gram equivalent weight per litre (6)
Isotonic (6)
Non-pathological—requiring no remedial action
Most frequently occurring (1)
Unmodified (?)
Mathematical average (2)

Script B
Relative to a majority state (1)

Script C
(a) The normal type is best fitted for his environment (3)
(b) The normal is average condition found in a large number of individuals (?2)
(c) The normal can be any standard form you may like to choose (4)
(d) Normal in any condition which has been found before (?)

(e) Normal is the simplest and most convenient condition found among many specimens (?1)

(f) A normal individual has all the essential characteristics of his species (?1)

Two hundred and eighty-three answers have been collected during six years (there is no compulsion for students to leave their scripts and several take them away). The scripts have been analysed to show the 'popularity'' of various meanings. Most of the meanings given can be classified into six areas of meaning and the percentage of scripts giving each of them is shown below.

Areas of meaning of 'normal' given:

	Percentage of scripts (total 283)
1. Usual, ordinary, common, like the majority, typical . .	72%
2. Average, mean	47%
3. Healthy, not diseased, sane, efficient, well adapted to purpose	25%
4. Conforming to standard or rule	21%
5. At right angles, perpendicular	18%
6. Technical term in physics and chemistry, meaning a particular standard (e.g. normal temperature and pressure; normal solution containing the equivalent weight of a substance in grams per litre)	13%

In script A all the statements except 'unmodified' fall easily into one of the six areas of meaning, but some of those in script C are difficult to classify. For instance, although (b) might be put in area 2 because it contains the word 'average' it is not quite clear whether it is synonymous with 'arithmetical' mean, or with 'common'; and (e) might be put in area 1, but it does not necessarily mean the condition of the majority, for the 'simplest' condition might be rare.

These three scripts give an impression of considerable variation between individuals. The percentage of students who listed each meaning was, however, remarkably constant from year to year. For instance, in six successive years statements were placed in area 1 by the following percentages: 68, 57, 70, 64, 83, 81; in area 2 by 48, 43, 43, 42, 55, 52; and 'sane', or 'mentally normal', a subdivision of area 3, by 4, 4, 6, 6, 8, 5 per cent of students.

The choice of meanings

The relative popularity of the areas of meaning seemed to have been determined by the situation in which the students were asked to make their lists. The areas of meaning most commonly given (1 and 2) were those most clearly relevant to the passage they had just read, and to their working at the time in an anatomy department. The 'physiological' or 'functional' meaning (3) was given by only a quarter of the students, although, as we shall see later, it became clear in discussion that their understanding of the word was strongly influenced by this meaning—it was at the back of their minds. The physical and chemical meanings (6) were quite well known to the students, but only one in seven listed them. When these meanings were produced in discussion, many people were surprised to find that they had just forgotten to mention them or that they had remembered them but assumed such meanings were not asked for. Some attempted to rule them out when others suggested them: 'surely these are extraneous, I mean, they're not in keeping with the word normal in its exact sense.' Sometimes there was laughter or jeering as though these contributions were regarded as outrageously inappropriate. It has happened at least twice that a student said that in making his list he had written these meanings down and then crossed them out because he thought they were not required.

Here we see how even when the context appeared to be fairly free, and the student was asked to give all the meanings he could think of, still he made a selection consciously or unconsciously, according to what seemed to be appropriate to the situation. While he was working on his own, studying the quotation, parts of his store of information were not being tapped. During discussion other parts became accessible when he saw that everybody had not made the same selection, and this reminded him of what had been overlooked. Here again we see how the group acts as a testing-ground to help to find more useful ways of behaving.

In order to bring this discussion of the receipt of verbal information into line with the earlier discussion on visual perception, we can describe the areas of meaning as schemata. The majority of the students will have had experience in the past of the word 'normal' being used with each of these areas of meaning, that is, they will all have these schemata as parts of their store of information. When asked to list all the definitions of normal they can think of, they make different selections from their store.

Dictionary definitions of normal

At this point we will see what authoritative statements have been made about the meanings of normal. I have consulted two general and four medical dictionaries, and have allocated their statements in the same way as the students', to our six areas of meaning.

Dictionary	Areas of meaning covered					
Webster's	1	2	3	4	5	6
Shorter Oxford	1	2		4	5	6
Stedman's Medical	1		3			
Blakiston's New Gould Medical		2	3	4		6
Dorland's Medical				4		6
Faber's Medical				4		6

Only Webster's covers the total pool of student's meanings; the Shorter Oxford omits 'healthy'. Three of the four medical dictionaries omit to give the two most popular of the students' meanings, but give the least popular.

The use of 'normal' in medical literature

The word 'normal' is of course widely used in scientific literature, and though I have not made a systematic search for its meanings, the following quotations are sufficient to indicate a divergence of opinion about the word very similar to that shown by the students.

D. M. Lyon (1942), in an article, '*What do we mean by "Normal"?*', in the Clinical Journal, says that, 'Normal does not merely mean average, but a range of values round the average. The simplest conception of normal is to think of it in relation to the Gaussian curve, and for medical purposes the range of normality is best expressed by $M. \pm 2$ S.D. Absence of disease is merely a secondary meaning which arises from the fact that the healthy state conforms to the Gaussian distribution.'

This author thus suggested a refinement of our area 1 as the most useful definition of normal, and regarded area 3 as secondary.

By contrast C. Daly King (1945), in an article on '*The Meaning of Normal*', in The Yale Journal of Biology and Medicine, objected to the ' . . . misuse of the term, normal, in a sense synonymous with "average" or "ordinary". . . . The average may be, and very often is, abnormal. The normal, on the other hand, is objectively, and properly, to be defined as *that which functions in accordance with its design*. . . . What is in fact normal can never be ascertained simply by the use of any mathematical tool, because its essential dependence is upon qualitative consideration, and mathematics deals with quantitative data . . . we propose to use normal and average as distinguishable contrasts and to define them as follows:—"average"—that which results from mathematical computation based upon more than one sample, i.e. a specimen mean, "normal"—that which functions in accordance with its inherent design, i.e. a pattern norm.'

This author would restrict 'normal' to our area 4, conforming to standards, and rejected areas 1 and 2.

C. W. Heath *et al.* (1945), in their book *What people are: a study of normal young men*, say that, 'The "Normal" individual, therefore, here is regarded as the balanced person whose combination of traits of all sorts allows him to function effectively in a variety of ways. This idea of "normal" is accordingly an elastic one. It does not restrict our studies to the statistically average person, nor does it project us into a vain search for the normal person in the sense of a "perfect" one. . . . The word "normal", therefore, is here given some of its original meaning of the perpendicular and the balanced.'

This definition would come in our area 3.

Jones (1942), discussing the *Concept of the Normal Mind*, says, 'In work of this order one feels little need to ponder on careful definitions of normality, and, if asked to produce one, it is easy to be content with such general phrases as "a mind functioning efficiently", "a healthy mind", "an organism well adapted to reality", "a personality achieving its maximum of happiness", "a personality in good contact with the social standards prevailing in the environment". All these phrases are useful at times and serve to recall to our mind certain standards of value; they prove quite adequate in practice for gross work in psychopathology. Reflection soon shows, however, that they one and all beg the question by assuming that something, e.g. efficiency or health, has been previously defined when in fact it had not.'

This definition also would come in area 3.

Of special interest to us is a paper by J. A. Ryle (1947) on 'The Meaning of Normal', for he showed how the meaning attributed to the word by physicians has affected their behaviour. He wrote, 'In medicine and the medical sciences the word "normal" is in constant use, but as a rule, without a proper clarification of its meaning . . . it is commonly held to be synonymous with "healthy", but health too awaits a better definition . . . physicians have refined their methods of detecting departures from the "normal" without first reviewing the idea of normal or discussing its limitations. In the Oxford English Dictionary normal is defined as "average" or "mean", or "not deviating or differing from a type or standard"; but that the normal, in biological usage is something other than a mean or fixed standard can scarcely be disputed. In man, as in all animals, variation is so constantly at work that no rigid pattern—whether anatomical, physiological or immunological—is possible.

'In consequence of the neglect of the study of "healthy" populations and of what may best be described as "normal variability", a number of physical findings due to clinical and associated methods have been accounted abnormal (in the sense of pathological) with quite inadequate justification and often for long periods. Inaccurate diagnoses, faulty treatments and unnecessary invalidism have again and again been traced to this failure in essential discipline.

' . . . Health and disease know no sharp boundary. They could only do so if it were possible for biology to adopt the dictionary definition of normality.'

Here we have again the confusion that arises if normal is equated with average (meaning arithmetical mean), or with a narrowly conceived fixed standard, any deviation from which is 'abnormal', i.e. correlated with ill-health. The 'normal' in biology and medicine according to Ryle is better expressed in terms of the range of variability within which efficient performance and adaptation to common stresses may be recognized. His definition would then fall within areas 1 and 3, and he points out the dangers of using the word as in areas 2 and 4.

An interesting passage occurs in *Instincts of the Herd in Peace and War*, by Trotter (1916), according to whom normal in the sense of the physician is 'no more than a statistical expression implying the condition of the average man. It could scarcely fail, however, to acquire the significance of "healthy". If once the statistically normal mind is accepted as being synonymous with the psychologically healthy mind (that is, the mind in which the full capacities are available for use), a standard is set up which has a most fallacious appearance of objectivity. The statistically normal mind can be regarded only as a mind which has responded in the usual way to the moulding and deforming influence of its environment—that is, to human standards of discipline, taste, and morality. If it is to be looked upon as typically healthy also, the current human standards of whose influence it is a product must necessarily be accepted as qualified to call forth the best in the developing mind they mould.'

Trotter also is interested in the strength of the tendency to equate the condition of the majority with the notion of healthy, and points out still other implications of this which are not easily recognized, namely the implication that the usual environmental conditions are also the optimal ones.

Finally, the following quotations are from a recent number of the British Journal of Psychology (1955). In a review by Metcalfe, of a philosophical discussion of the psychological notion of normal behaviour (*La notion de normal en Psychologie clinique*. By Fr. Duyckaerts) we are told, 'The author chooses to discuss normality first as "integration", then as "autonomy" in relation to other individuals, as "adaptation" to different social groups, and finall as resemblance to the average . . . to be normal, behaviour must be purposeful . . . it must be creative . . . it must include an assimilation of the past and of surrounding cultural values and aim at the building up of effective social contact. The concept of normality identified with statistical average is rejected with horror. Kant is called in to help in the forty-page demonstration that such heresy does not fulfil any of the criteria of a logical definition, and in a mood of angry humour the author attempts to unveil the motives of those whom he believes to uphold such a notion.'

In the same journal there is a review of a book (*Growing up in the City*, by Mays, 1955) by Mack, who says that 'this is a first-class study of "normal" delinquency, that is delinquency socially determined, connoting no personal instability in the delinquent. . . .'

I shall not attempt to allocate such heavily loaded definitions as these to any of our six areas.

The group as a microcosm

One has the impression that if the writers quoted above took part in a discussion on the word 'normal' in the same kind of conditions as the students did, they could not avoid getting involved in the same disagreements, nor would they argue more dispassionately. These writers have given deliberate thought to the way other people use the word normal, and to what they think is a suitable use, indeed three of them have taken the trouble to write a whole article about it. Although the students have probably never before deliberately pondered on the word, there is nevertheless reproduced in any one group of twelve, the same varieties of meaning as the experts have crystallized out for themselves. I think we would find this to be so if we discussed many other terms which are currently used in biology such as 'primitive', 'fundamental', 'environmental', 'inherited'. Any one group of these students then can be regarded as a kind of microcosm, reflecting however imperfectly or naïvely, the current attitudes of biologists and medical men, sharing the same scientific culture. This is one reason why my own interest in the discussions rarely flagged even after having listened to more than fifty of them.

During discussion the participants use the word in one or other of its senses and it becomes clear that the use of a word with so many meanings gives rise to some confusion, both in attempting to communicate unambiguously with each other and in attempting to think clearly themselves.

Confusion in communication

An illustration of how communication between people can be made difficult by using a word such as normal is given by the case of an old man whose illness could not be diagnosed for some days after he had entered hospital. On admission he had been asked if his diet was normal and had replied yes. After some time one of the physicians asked what exactly had he been eating, and when this question was put, the patient said he had been eating little more than bread, margarine and treacle during the last three years. It then became clear that he was suffering from scurvy, a possibility which had not been entertained (although the signs were present, they were not perceived) until it was known that his diet had been deficient in vitamin C. In asking the patient if his diet was normal, the questioner had wanted to know if his diet was suitable to maintain health; in saying that his diet was normal the patient had wanted to say that there had been no recent change from his usual diet.

This is an example where the questioner failed to obtain the information he required because different people attributed alternative meanings to the same word. This danger can be easily avoided by substituting words which are less likely to be differently interpreted by the two parties, but a second danger is not so easily recognized or avoided.

Confusion in thinking

The second danger is that the multiple meanings confuse one's own thinking, and as Ryle and Trotter have pointed out may affect behaviour inappropriately. Here the danger arises not so much because alternative interpretations are possible as because the meanings overlap and contaminate each other without our recognizing it. Some of the meanings—for instance the technical terms of areas 5 and 6—do not cause much difficulty in this way, because the context usually prescribes them definitively. In using the term 'normal body' in anatomy, one is not likely to be confused by the meaning appropriate to 'normal aliphatic hydrocarbon'. On the other hand one is likely to be confused by the physiological sense of normal, that is, healthy, as the following analysis of how the areas of meaning are interrelated will elucidate.

In describing a man's height as normal we are using the word in sense 1, like the majority, or perhaps 2, approximating to the mean; what is 'normal' in this case is determined empirically, and the word does not necessarily have the connotation of 'desirable'. However, deviations from the commonly occurring condition may be undesirable or inconvenient (as Ryle pointed out, a tall man is more likely to sustain a head injury in low doorways). It is indeed difficult to think of normal without having 'abnormal' also in mind, so even the apparently restricted meanings 1 and 2 tend to take the connotation of desirable by contrast. Meaning 3, healthy, etc., cannot avoid having a favourable connotation. Meanings 1 and 3, however, overlap (as Trotter indicated) because in fact the majority of people are also healthy and indeed deviation of any feature, such as pulse rate, from the condition of the majority, may be a sign of disease. Meaning 4, 'conforming to a standard' shares with 1 an ambiguity as to desirability according to whether the standard is established empirically or arbitrarily.

To analyse still further some of the confusion of thinking, we can see that it is not only the overlapping of meanings that gives rise to difficulty, but the tendency to go beyond the accepted meanings of the word into their implications. This was brought out clearly by Trotter, when he said that when the statistically normal mind is regarded as synonymous with the psychologically healthy mind, it is implied that the conditions under which such a mind is produced must be regarded as the best. This brings out clearly that a word like 'normal' has not only a number of separate meanings which are sufficiently clearly defined to be given in a dictionary, but also has a number of associations which ramify through many kinds of areas not at first sight connected. The organizations of schemata are complex, and we are to a large extent unaware of their interactions with each other.

In defence of vagueness

Although the interactions cause confusion in some cases, it must not be thought that they are always disadvantageous; on the contrary, they may help to make available parts of our store of experience in a way that precise words cannot. We may usefully refer again to our schemata for apples; these are built up from information received through various sense organs during intimate traffic with apples as we grow, buy, sell or eat them, and such schemata may give us exquisite sensibility in distinguishing apples of specific, named, catalogued varieties. But such clearly prescribed schemata may be related, more or less tenuously, to others concerning apple blossom, apple weevil, the apple of discord or of my eye, and the Garden of Eden; and for any one person to follow these associations would lead him far and wide and deep into his own life history. All sorts of information otherwise locked up in separate chambers of the treasury of his experience would become available to him. As we saw (p. 52), inventive or imaginative work in science depends on having schemata which can be flexibly associated in this tenuous way. In developing language for scientific purposes, we need to keep in mind the value of words of many meanings in facilitating the association of schemata, a function which a technical language consisting only of words of precise and unambiguous meaning cannot so easily serve.

Usually we have no control over the associations of schemata, because we are mostly unaware of them; it is suggested here that conscious scrutiny of these associations will help to weed out those that are not useful.

The process of discussion

The discussions were concerned with unravelling the complex effects of the meanings on each other, and with understanding the difficulty of isolating them. Working at the exercise on their own, most of the students had felt that their understanding of the paragraph from the textbook of anatomy was clear and sound; that is, from the total pool of meanings known to him, each had selected to his own satisfaction, what he had thought the most appropriate in this particular context. But to varying extents, not recognized until it became clearer in discussion, some other meanings had influenced the understanding of different people in various ways. It was very difficult to get agreement on how the passage might be rewritten to express unambiguously what each person thought the author intended to say. This reflected the difficulty of agreeing on how areas of meaning should be isolated. There seemed to be a great reluctance to restrict or localize the meaning of the word even when it was allowed that confusion resulted. Although it was recognized that 'normal' is a vague word, and some went so far as to say it should be abandoned, there was considerable resistance to the suggestion that it should be replaced with terms of fewer meanings, for instance that 'commonly occurring type' should replace 'normal type' in the given passage. It seemed that the students preferred to use words of richer meanings, even if they are ambiguous, than more narrowly defined ones, just as they preferred to make inferences, even if of doubtful validity, rather than factual statements about the hand radiographs. This phenomenon is perhaps related to the 'effort after meaning', the tendency referred to previously (pp. 89, 90), to try to extract as much information as possible from a given event. This point we shall examine again later in connection with classification.

What did we hope the students would take away from the discussion on 'normal' apart from the experience that the attempt to understand words can be exciting, tedious and frustrating? We hoped that they would realize that the receipt of information from words involves the same kind of processes of selection and interpretation as does receipt of information from a visual pattern; and that some understanding of the factors affecting these processes might help them to use language with greater effectiveness.

Could this not be done more quickly and less painlessly by letting them listen to a lecture on semantics? This question was often asked by students in the discussions, and was answered by others, in such terms as 'It's one thing to be told about the mistakes other people make, it's quite a different thing to discover how you make them yourself'. To quote from a student's essay: 'There is no better way of getting hold of a point than by forgetting it, not realizing it, or making a mistake over it and then having the feeling of ignorance and stupidity attended by listening to others discussing it as though it were the most obvious thing in the world to notice or do.' (Johnson, 1950.)

The kind of change which has to be effected is the reassessing and rearranging of what is already in the mind, rather than the receiving of new packets of 'facts', and this is a change which has to be made by the student for himself. The role of the teacher is a modest one—that of arranging conditions to facilitate this change.

8

Classifying

THE discussion on classification, the fifth in the course, followed naturally on the discussion of 'normal', for describing and naming are closely associated with classifying. In using the word 'normal' one is automatically dividing the population into two classes, normal and abnormal. One is also conveying information about other members of the group to which the thing can be allocated. If you say the height of a man is 5 ft. 6 in. you are giving information about the man in isolation: if you say his height is normal you are referring him, as far as height is concerned, to his position in a population and, reciprocally, you are giving information about the height of the majority of that particular population. For this reason to say that a man's height is normal is often more 'interesting' and 'meaningful' than to say that it is 5 ft. 6 in.

The students prepared for this discussion by writing a short essay on classification. This task was a less restricted one than those which preceded the discussions on hand radiographs and the word 'normal', and gave greater freedom to exploring stores of information; consequently it is not so easy to identify common themes in the various groups. Except for the controversy over 'absolute' systems of classification, to which I shall refer below, this topic did not confront the students, as the previous ones did, with a sharp challenge to their accustomed ways of thinking. Discussion tended to be concerned with digestion of the lessons of previous discussion, with re-ordering the material under a new title, and discovering the importance of classification for thinking. Unfortunately the thoughtful and stimulating analysis of classification (or categorization) by Bruner, Goodnow and Austin (1956), was not available to us; we should have profited much from their formulations of some of the aspects we discussed.

The following points were readily agreed upon by most students. We tend to associate like things with each other, making a sort of filing system for convenient arrangement of knowledge. This is done more or less automatically, continuously, and from our earliest days. The criteria we use consciously or unconsciously for classification vary with our purpose, that is, we select certain properties of a thing and ignore others, according to convenience; thus we may arrange books according to size, or colour, or author, or subject, or date of publication. Different systems of classification may cross each other, that is, an item may be placed in several classes. Systems of classification, for instance of flowering plants, are continually modified as a result of further research.

Some of the confusions in using the word 'normal' were seen to arise from inadequate definitions of the class to which the thing so described was allocated. A man who is 5 ft. 6 in. tall may be of normal height in England, but if he went among the pygmies of central Africa he would not be. The kind of statement frequently made in discussing the word 'normal' was that 'a lunatic may be normal in a mental home, but you can't really call him normal, can you?' There is a double confusion here. In sense 1 (see page 99) a lunatic can be said to be normal or like the majority in a mental hospital, but not normal or like the majority outside it, i.e., he is being referred to two different populations, and is normal or not normal according to the population. The second confusion arises because though he may be normal in sense 1 within the mental home population he is not normal in sense 3, healthy.

Although many agreed on the man-made nature of classificatory systems, and recognized that they were arbitrary and subject to modification according to human convenience, the feeling was often expressed that there must also be an 'absolute' system of classification, which does not depend on human convenience, which exists apart from man's conceptions, and is perfect, permanent and unchanging.

Miss A expressed the idea thus:

'. . . in certain fields at any rate, there is a fundamental classification which is . . . which always has existed and doesn't really depend on how you yourself split it up, it is not a purely man-made thing.'

And later:

'No I don't think that . . . classification is man made, and of course it has, it has to be discovered but, I, I think that in chemistry there is a fundamental order of things and . . . perhaps in biology one might be discovered.'

In another group *Mr. B.* expressed the same idea more forcibly:

'Firstly, I quite agree with the personal classification which is, I think, an arbitrary one. Secondly, I can fully visualize two people coming together and creating a classification for their mutual benefit. But thirdly, I do insist that there must be an absolute classification, which is absolutely invariable, and is a product of the order of things.'

In still another group the matter was discussed in the following way:

Mr. C: An absolute system would only occur when you had absolute knowledge.'

Mr. D: 'If we look at it from so to speak the eyes of God . . . who can see everything from the beginning to the end so to speak . . . there must be a basic sort of classification taking everything into account. I mean when He knows everything and all so to speak. . . . As Mr. C says, when we have absolute knowledge, then we shall have an absolute classification.'

Mr. E: 'Even if you do have absolute knowledge of everything at any one time things are always changing and you always get new types, so you could never—you would never . . . it'd be out of date almost as soon as you'd got it.'

Mr. F: 'Well that wouldn't . . .'

Mr. G: 'That wouldn't be absolute knowledge. . . .'

Mr. D: 'That wouldn't be . . .'

Mr. G: 'You're denying the term you've premised, aren't you? If you say that you've got absolute knowledge you've got absolute knowledge and that means you know everything about the given topic and you know . . .'

Mr. E: 'I'm sorry I thought . . .'

Mr. G: '. . . the changes, you can forecast the changes, etc.'

Mr. E: '. . . I thought you meant absolute knowledge at a given time.'

Mr. F: 'Yes, but even if absolute knowledge were achieved different groups of people would be applying that knowledge for different purposes in which case they'd be using their various classifications for their own particular purpose.'

Mr. D: 'But they are using a classification which is there for them to use, if you see what I mean.'

This discussion went on for some time, *Mr. D* struggling to make his meaning clear, the others intently concentrating on trying to understand him. ('You can practically hear the brains ticking over,' someone listening to the record said.) This was the record referred to on page 70 which provoked first laughter, and then serious attention, in another group listening to it.

Miss A, *Mr. B* and *Mr. D* were expressing the nineteenth-century view that science is concerned with 'a world of external nature, sharply distinguished from subjective illusions, whose course, observable by the senses, is the result of the operation on inert matter of universal unalterable laws deducible by reason', whereas the modern view regards 'the achievements of science as the discovery of relations between our experiences' (Dingle, 1951). Bruner, Goodnow and Austin, 1956, discussing 'the invention of categories', also refer to this point:

'For Newton, science was a voyage of discovery on an uncharted sea. The objective of the voyage was to discover the islands of truth. The truths existed in nature. Contemporary science has been hard put to shake the yoke of this dogma. Science and common-sense inquiry alike do not discover the ways in which events are grouped in the world; they invent ways of grouping.'

Such strongly held belief about how the physical world 'must' be organized, the feeling that it 'must' be fixed and eternally stable, not subject to the whim of man, affected the way the student received information from the course of discussions. It is related to very generalized and long-established assumptions about the relation of oneself to the external physical world. The belief was challenged at many points in the course, by the illustrations of the

projective nature of visual perception, or by the demonstration
that the word 'normal' has no 'intrinsic' meaning, only a number
of usages, for example. Different students seemed to feel the
impact of the challenge most strongly over different topics, or at
different rates; for different students, different rational topics
made perceptible associations with these basic, generalized
schemata or assumptions. A student who has passed through
even the 'normal' discussion without apparent trauma might find
the one on classification altogether too much to stomach; an
example is given at some length later (see p. 134–138).

Extrapolation and prediction

To continue with the points about classification on which
students agreed; it was clear that it can do far more than help
us to keep things tidy. It can give us more information than we
have at the moment direct access to—that is, it helps us to
extrapolate and to predict.

A famous example of this can be cited from chemistry. The
system of classification of the elements according to atomic weight
and chemical properties devised by Mendeléef was such that he
was able to predict the discoveries of certain elements not at that
time known. It is interesting to note that when Newlands, three
years earlier than Mendeléef, attempted a similar classification,
he was ridiculed, a member of a learned society inquiring whether
he had thought of classifying the elements according to their
initial letters (Taylor, 1932). Such a question implies that one
system of classification is as good as any other as long as one
knows the rules, and this may be so as far as one function of
classification is concerned, that of making a tidy arrangement of
a large number of various things. But it is not true as far as the
second and in many cases more important function of classification
is concerned, that of helping us to extrapolate and predict.

A second example of how classification allows extrapolation
is provided by biology. Linnaeus invented a convenient filing
system for animals and plants, using certain arbitrarily chosen
criteria. He believed that each species had been created individually and that his arrangement reflected a scheme in the mind
of the Creator. But the classification he had devised was such that
Darwin some hundred years later saw something new in it—

evidence for the theory of common descent. When Linnaeus placed together several different species in one genus, and separated them from another group of species in a different genus, he was indicating his estimate of degrees of similarity. Just as a potter might use a variety of moulds, some more similar than others, the Creator had used a variety of patterns, some more like than others, to make animals and plants. Darwin saw that the different degrees of similarity might result from different degrees of blood relationship. The diverse organisms constituting one genus might have arisen more recently from a common stock than had the more diverse organisms constituting several genera. From classification of animals and plants then, we get information about what probably happened in the near or distant past.

At a humbler level we are all continually making use of this property of classification of giving us information additional to that got from direct inspection. In diagnosis the doctor sees certain signs and receives an account of certain symptoms directly from the patient. These he regards as indications that the disease is of a certain kind or class—he gives it a name. If he has correctly classified the patient, made the correct hypothesis, he knows a great deal more about him than he has been able to find out himself in the clinical examination; for instance, that it is likely that there are certain germs in his blood, certain substances in his urine. He can extrapolate in this way because it has been found that in many other cases these conditions tend to occur together, to be correlated with each other. Moreover the doctor can predict that certain things will happen in the future; that the patient's temperature will probably fall after three days, that spots will appear of a certain colour, size, shape and distribution, or that the patient will react in certain ways to certain drugs. The doctor, in making these extrapolations or predictions, is exploiting his own and other people's schemata of similar cases. He is saying in effect that because the patient is like certain others in certain perceivable respects, he is like them in many others. If he has placed the patient in the right class, that is, made a correct diagnosis, his extrapolations and predictions will be borne out; if he has made an incorrect diagnosis, they will not be. At a still humbler level we exploit classification in the same way when we choose an apple, classifying it consciously or unconsciously as one that will be crisp to the bite, or will cook satisfactorily, or will store well.

The most useful classification then is one which places together things which are alike in as many ways as possible, because the probability that they will be alike in other respects that we need to know about, but cannot know directly, will be greater. Methods of classification are continually being refined. For instance, certain patients diagnosed as having pneumonia did not respond to the antibacterial treatment which was successful in the majority of cases; that is, they had in common with pneumonia patients features a, b, c, d, e, f, which can be seen in clinical examination, but not feature g—response to antibacterial drugs. It is likely that these aberrant pneumonia cases differed in other respects than g, and the problem was to find some other feature that could be used more quickly and easily than response to treatment with antibacterial drugs, the testing of which may waste time. These aberrant cases, it was found, could be distinguished by serological tests, which show that the infective agent is a virus, but the tests could not be used quickly enough to aid in diagnosis and treatment (Crofton *et al.*, 1951).

To relate the discussion on classification to those on visual perception: the information we derive from any stimulus pattern —as we saw in Chapters 1–3 and again in discussing hand radiographs—is compounded of information that can be checked against the stimulus pattern, and information which cannot be directly checked. The information we get from present stimulation has a high probability of being valid, or at any rate it can be tested directly, either by repeating or checking our own observations, or getting somebody else to do so. Even such information is subject to modification according to what class we have placed the object in. Though it is in most circumstances true that 'a rose by any other name would smell as sweet' it is not invariably so; the name or class we give an object does affect our perception of it, because it affects the choice of schemata which come into operation. As long as the information received is testable by acting on it, however, we are likely to get information of predictable value.

The information derived in this more direct way from the object is only part, however, of the information we react to. We react also to information obtained much less directly, from the more distantly related schemata which come into association with the more immediately relevant ones. We tend to pick up certain clues which help us to relate the object to its class: we tend to think that if a thing is like other members of the class in certain respects which we can test, it is like them in all other significant respects, many of which we do not test. Indeed, for many of the most useful respects we cannot yet test, because they are concerned with future events. In medicine, it is clearly the future of the patient that concerns us—what the present condition tells us about what will happen, sooner or later. When, as in diagnosis, we act upon information got by extrapolation, then it is very important which class we put the object in.

In naming and classifying then, we find the same principles as in seeing: the information gained is partly contributed by ourselves from our past experience of similar things; indeed when we classify a thing, we are deciding which of our schemata are appropriate to it. It is important that we recognize that information obtained indirectly by classifying does not have the same degree of validity as that obtained directly. We shall, however, increase its validity if we consider alternative possibilities of classification, and by further testing of information directly obtainable from the object, seek confirmation and non-confirmation of our guesses as to the class in which the object is most appropriately placed.

Analogy

Certain visual illusions can be explained if we assume that we automatically tend to consider that things that are similar in certain respects are similar in all or many others. Thus, when we look at two lighted balloons in an otherwise darkened room, one expanding and the other contracting, we see the first rushing towards us and the other receding away (Kilpatrick, 1952). We have assumed that the balloons, similar in many respects, are of the same size, and explain the difference in size of the images by assuming difference of distance. When we argue by analogy we treat things that we know to be unlike in some ways though alike in others, as similar in still other respects. The well-recognized danger of using analogies is the tendency to push them too far—

to treat the two things as like in respects in which they are in fact
unlike, so that we get something comparable with a visual illusion,
non-valid information. The processes involved in making analogies
are similar to those involved in classifying, and the advantages and
dangers are also similar.

Patterns and aesthetic judgment

During the history of the development of any classificatory
system the succession of people concerned in its making may not
have had any inkling of the kind of new information that might
some time emerge. They seem rather to have been activated by a
feeling that certain arrangements are in themselves more fitting,
suitable or satisfying than others, as Newlands thought that to
arrange elements by atomic weight was more appropriate than to
arrange them by their initial letters. Darwin (1859) saw how his
predecessors had unconsciously or intuitively perceived such a
pattern as would allow him later to formulate a general law in
explanation of that pattern:

'. . . community of descent is the hidden bond which naturalists
have been unconsciously seeking, and not some unknown plan of
creation, or the enunciation of general propositions, and the mere
putting together and separating objects more or less alike.'

Here again we see how the same stimulus pattern is
differently interpreted by different people according to the schemata
they associate with it.

Judgment of the suitability of a system of classification is
presumably based on the perception, not necessarily conscious, of
a pattern of correlated features, and seems to involve the same
kind of processes of aesthetic judgment. One may be able sooner
or later to justify logically the preferment of one arrangement
above another, but the stage of formulation is often preceded by
a general vague feeling of unease, a notion that there is something
wrong somehow with one arrangement. Similarly it often happens
on reading a faulty argument that one does not immediately know
in what way it is faulty or whether indeed it really is, but it
just 'smells' wrong. It would seem in such cases that the new
information makes an ill-fitting match with rather generalized
schemata of which one is hardly aware.

9

Evaluating Evidence

So far in the discussion course we had been considering behaviour in which no deliberate effort of judgment seems to be made, though the receipt of information has been accompanied automatically by an act of judgment, or selection and interpretation. In the present chapter we are concerned with the factors that affect more conscious acts of judgment, of the kind a doctor or scientist has to make frequently, and knows he has to make, namely whether or not a certain hypothesis has been supported by the results of an experiment. To bring such behaviour into line with what we have been discussing previously, we may say that the scientist is concerned with getting information of predictive value from an experiment.

The sixth discussion of the course was concerned with the factors that affect the information received from the report of an experiment. It is, of course, well recognized that aesthetic, ethical, religious or political opinions may bias judgment on matters to which such opinions may seem to be (to other people) strictly speaking irrelevant; a famous case is the controversy over the theory of evolution.

Scientists try to free themselves from extraneous factors, such as these, which affect their judgment about scientific matters. But many unrecognized factors of a more subtle kind influence the assessment of evidence, as became clear in the discussion.

The students first read a paper published in a scientific journal reporting a biological experiment and the conclusions drawn from it. They then answered the following questions:

1. Quote a statement which summarizes what the author claims she has discovered.

119

2. Compare this with the observations actually made.
3. How would *you* set out to test the hypothesis that ' . . .'
(The author's hypothesis was stated.)

The students' answers to the third question showed that they
had a good grasp of experimental method, and understood the
need to standardize conditions, change only one significant
variable at a time, and set up adequate controls. But they did not
apply these stringent requirements to the experimental evidence
presented in the paper. In order to test how they had assessed
the author's claim, they were asked whether they would expect
that their own experiments would support the hypothesis, that is,
whether their animals would react in the same way as the author
reported hers had. Most of them thought they certainly would,
some thought the chances were even and a few thought that their
animals would behave in the opposite way, having it seemed
taken a great dislike to the paper. Thus, given the same report,
the students had received different information from it, had made
varying assessments of the validity of the author's claims.

In discussion it appeared that the factors that had influenced
their judgment ranged from features of the immediate situation
that could be easily altered, to deeply rooted personality characteristics, i.e., schemata of a generalized, long-established kind.
For instance, some said that they were naturally more critical of
the article in the class-room, where they were supposed to be
learning to be critical, than they would have been if they had
casually picked up the journal in the common-room. Their attitude
depended on their geographical position at the moment. This
factor is comparable with the relative positions of the two shapes
which affect our estimate of their size (pp. 30, 32).

An example of a less transient factor was their assessment of
the status of the writer. Many were impressed by the fact that
the paper was published in what is usually regarded as a reputable
journal, and were consequently uncritical of the vagueness of the
report and the inadequacy of the experimental design. Some
students had noted that the author was a woman, an American,
and that though the experiments were on nutrition, she wrote
from a department concerned with a different aspect of biology.
According to whether they regarded such omens as indicating

good or bad research potentiality they had assessed the evidence presented more, or less, favourably. These factors are less easily changed than geographical situation, but one might expect them to be modified with increasing experience of research publications, that is, improvement of their schemata relating to journals.

Much deeper, still less easily changed factors that had affected judgment were concerned with the students' generalized schemata concerning human nature. Some thought that people can be,.and should be, trusted to do good work and to tell the truth; that one should always put the best possible interpretation on statements even if they were vague and confused and should assume that certain necessary precautions had been taken even if they were not described. Others thought that one must always be on one's guard against being taken in. Some did not like to be harsh, others thought that scientists must be sceptical. The clashes of opinion that resulted were often quite serious.

As with other topics, the discussions of this article followed very much the same lines from group to group and year to year, and the points noted above as having affected judgment can be regarded as being of very wide occurrence among medical students. It is important to note that some of the factors became apparent only as a result of prolonged discussion. Judgment had been made very quickly (only twenty minutes was allowed for the whole exercise including the design of the experiment), but had been determined by this enormously complex interacting mass of factors. It was sometimes disturbing to students to find that their judgment on a straightforward scientific matter had been influenced among other things, by whether in general they trusted people. In this discussion more than in any other of the series did it become clear that if one is to improve one's judgment in scientific matters, habits of thought which had seemed to belong to a quite separate field of behaviour must also be changed.

Patterns again

As with seeing, the judging of evidence from a written passage involves interpretation. From the material presented, such information is taken in as is felt to be most consistent, to make the most suitable pattern, both with the immediate context, and with the recipient's store of information. Again we see, as with selecting the meanings of 'normal' (p. 100), or with choosing criteria for classification (p. 118), our behaviour is affected by a kind of aesthetic appreciation of what is most appropriate to the particular circumstances. The data are not assessed in isolation, but in relation to other things which may be, or may not be, strictly speaking relevant.

Examples of how this manner of behaving can be exploited is provided by many advertisements. A pertinent one which currently appears in periodicals consists of two parts. One part, the text, states that worrying is mainly a matter of 'nerves', and refers to the beneficial effects of the tonic advertised on the metabolism of nerve cells. Adjacent to the text is a picture of some part of the nervous system, a touch receptor, a section of nerve, nerve endings terminating in muscle fibres, or what not, with a caption. The text does not usually refer to the picture, nor does the caption of the picture refer to the text, but the reader tends to interpret the advertisement as a whole. It cannot be supposed that the picture gives information of much medical importance to the layman reader, for it is not clear how big these things are, or where exactly they are, or how many of each he might harbour, but presumably the picture, simply by being adjacent to the text, serves to give the hallmark of authority to the medical recommendation of the text, as did the name of the journal to the article discussed above. It is as though the reader is expected to think that the tonic must be good because the advertisers seem to know such a lot about nerve cells, and perhaps the diagrams are the more suitable for this purpose, the more incomprehensible to the layman they are.

Relevance and irrelevance

We see then that in making a judgment about experimental evidence a large number of factors have played a part. For any one person's judgment, all these factors can be described as relevant—in the sense that they have been influential. They may have helped or hindered the student to come to a useful decision, that is, to get information of predictive value. What is usually regarded as relevant is that which tends to lead to the correct judgment. Thus, of the factors which were shown to have affected the students' judgment, their geographical position would be irrelevant, because as often as not it would lead them to the wrong judgment. But the presence of the report in a certain journal would be relevant. In most cases they would be justified in being favourably disposed to the evidence presented in a reputable journal, because papers are usually subjected to criticism by colleagues before being submitted for publication, and by the editor and referees before being accepted. They were therefore assuming that they could rely on the opinions of people more experienced than themselves, who had approved the publication.

In everyday life we are continually evaluating evidence, though we may not be aware of making any judgment. For instance, many of us tend to believe more or less without question much of what we read in the newspaper, or at least to think there is some truth in it. We have not, however, refrained from making a judgment in this case. We naturally choose to read a paper we trust rather than one we do not, and we have as it were, made a judgment by selection of the authority even before we read the material.

Causation

The discussion which followed the one on evaluation of evidence was closely linked with it, and concerned problems of causation. It was introduced by the students reading part of an article (Gregg, 1949) which discusses the effect on medicine, during the last seventy years, of the idea that each disease has its single and specific cause. As with other assumptions, the idea has been useful; it has enabled us to control such diseases as hydrophobia, typhoid and diphtheria. On the other hand its very success in such fields had inhibited developments in others; it has led to the comparative neglect of diseases for which a single sufficient cause cannot be found, and of consideration of the 'patient as a whole'. Since the article was written more and more attention has been paid to those aspects of medicine in which the notion of the single cause is not so useful. Already in 1944, for instance, the Goodenough Committee on medical education recommended that study of social and psychological medicine should be early integrated into the course. The students are prone, therefore, to consider the paper out of date, and what is interesting is that they nevertheless went on talking as though the notion of a single cause was deeply embedded in their thinking. Several referred, for instance, to the kind of patient who keeps coming to the doctor when there is 'nothing at all the matter with him', that is, when he has no infective agent in his system. They often equated 'disease' with infective agent or germ, saying for instance, that a man may have the disease in his throat, but be perfectly well.

The author of the paper, Gregg, describes the concept of a single cause as 'an idea so general and all-pervasive that it escaped explicit attention'. The paper therefore provided another example of the way our behaviour is influenced by our unquestioned assumptions, and discussion of it acted as a general summing up of one of the most important principles brought out in the course.

10

The Effects of the Discussion Course

THE aim of the course described was to help students to make sounder judgments about scientific matters, and it is necessary to inquire whether in fact it did so, especially in view of the unorthodox nature of the teaching technique used. Evidence about the effects of the course was obtained in two ways—by comparing the behaviour under examination conditions of students who had taken the course with that of others who had not, but were otherwise similar, and by studying what students said they felt about it.

The results of tests

During the last three years, half of the class took the course during the first term, and the other half during the second. At the end of the first term both halves of the class were given some tests in observation and reasoning, and significant differences were found between the two halves, which indicated that the course had had favourable effects on those who had taken it (James *et al.*, 1956). In their responses to the tests, the taught and and control parts of the class differed in the following four respects:

1. *Descriptions and inferences.* It will be recalled that when asked to list the differences between radiographs of two hands, many students did not recognize the difference between descriptions and inferences (pp. 85, 87). A descriptive statement is defined as one that can be confirmed by reference to the radiographs alone without any additional information. An inferential statement is one that involves extrapolation; it cannot be confirmed (or rejected) without additional information not present in the radiographs. One of the tests given resembled the hand radiograph

exercise; it consisted of a pair of radiographs (one of a normal, the other of a diseased chest) and the students were asked to list the differences between them. The taught students made more descriptive statements and fewer inferential statements than the controls.

This indicates that the course helped students to distinguish better between what can be tested with the material supplied and what cannot; between information obtained directly and that obtained from their store; in other words, between the real and the imaginary. Moreover, fewer taught students made inferences without giving the evidence for them, that is, without describing the appearance on the radiograph which had led them to make the statement, so that others could check the validity of the inference.

2. *True and false inferences*. It will have been clear from the discussion of the hand radiographs (pp. 85, 86) that descriptive statements are less interesting and useful than inferences. It is inferences that lead to action; a doctor who makes only a list of signs and symptoms, however accurate and comprehensive, without coming to any conclusions about diagnosis, is not being very helpful. We do not want to train students to be over-cautious and to refrain from making inferences lest they make mistakes, but we want them to distinguish better between correct and incorrect inferences. Helping them to understand the difference between descriptive and inferential statements is a means to this end.

The results of the test showed that the numbers of students making true inferences were not significantly different in the two halves of the class. This is as one might expect, because the making of correct inferences required anatomical knowledge (or good luck), and there is no reason to suppose that the two halves of the class would differ in this respect. But fewer among the taught half made false inferences, and this seems to indicate that the course had made them more critical of evidence.

3. *Alternative inferences*. In the chest radiograph test described above students were not specifically asked to make inferences because we wanted to see whether there was a difference in the kind of statement the two parts of the class spontaneously made: in the second test they were asked to do so, because we wanted to

see whether the discussions had helped students to consider more than one possible inference. This test consisted of two radiographs of a shoulder, one with the arm hanging straight down, the other with it turned inwards. The students were asked to describe the differences in appearance, and to state what they concluded was the position of the humerus (arm bone) in the two radiographs.

Three kinds of answer were given, correct (the arm is rotated inwards), incorrect (the arm is rotated outwards) and indeterminate (the arm is rotated). To make the correct inference (other than by good luck) it was necessary to have sufficient knowledge of anatomy to identify the parts of the humerus when seen from different aspects and to estimate that the degree of displacement shown could have occurred only by internal and not by external rotation. Again we would not expect the taught students either to be more lucky or to know more anatomy than the others, so we would not expect more of them to get the answer right, and they did not. But we would expect more of them to consider explicitly the two alternative inferences, so that they could deliberately weigh the evidence. In fact we found that three times as many students in the taught half, compared with the control, explicitly referred to two inferences. This we regard as more effective behaviour, because given a sufficient knowledge of anatomy the likelihood of getting the right answer is greater.

4. 'Set.' It is an advantage to approach each problem as a new one using previous experience in a critical manner, instead of blindly applying the method or ideas used in one problem to the next, where they may be inappropriate. By arranging problems in similar pairs it was possible to test the effect of one problem on a second. The shoulder test just described was followed immediately by a test on radiographs of two forearms in which the differences were due not to rotation as in the shoulder, but to a malformation of the elbow joint. When a student interpreted the differences in the forearm radiographs in terms of rotation, we considered that he was using his experience of the shoulder test inappropriately, employing the schema he used for one test uncritically for the next. (Analogous behaviour in medical practice would be, when a doctor having just diagnosed chicken-pox in one patient, diagnoses it again in the next patient who is actually

suffering from smallpox.) The number of students showing 'set' in this way was smaller in the taught than in the control parts of the class. We think that this shows that the discussions increase flexibility of behaviour.

To summarize, it seems from these tests that the discussions did effect some changes in behaviour of students in the desired direction; that is, they helped them to make sounder judgments. It is important to note that these changes were not brought about by intensive practising on material similar to that used for the tests: problems of interpretation of radiography were dealt with specifically only in the first discussion, fourteen weeks before the testing. It seems likely that the changes were of a generalized kind, and would affect other kinds of behaviour, for example, reasoning from experimental results, but we were not able to investigate this.

The reactions of the students

The other source of evidence about the effects of the course is the behaviour of students. The reaction of students to the course was naturally not always favourable. Attendance was optional, but very few people stayed away (of 278 students on the register in the last four years, 68 per cent were present at all eight discussions, and 86 per cent at seven or eight). There were, however, varying degrees of absenteeism among those who came, ranging from day-dreaming to the exhibition of boredom and disapproval, and it seems unlikely that people who were not quite with us, as it were, benefited much from being present. It must not be supposed, however, that all silent people did not learn; a student who had scarcely opened his mouth wrote an essay which showed very good understanding of the aims of the course.

As has been discussed in Chapter 5, many criticisms that were made indicated the difficulties of adjustment to a new kind of teaching method, where responsibility was deliberately transferred to the student. The commonest complaint was that the discussions were not sufficiently well disciplined, and that a lot of time was wasted through lack of chairmanship. People who liked talking were allowed to talk too much, and the quiet ones were not given a chance. There were criticisms too about my leaving the room while the exercise preceding the discussion was being done, and about having to write notes for this. Some students complained that the aims were not made clear at a sufficiently early stage. This, I think, is the familiar difficulty of 'seeing' something new. In practice, I always made a point of stating the aims as clearly as I was able, but this was no guarantee that they were understood.

The most common favourable statement students made about the course was that it made them think. Many have said that the class discussion itself only started the process. A point of interest about the students' personal reactions is that realization of the effect seems sometimes to have been considerably delayed. Several students told me on meeting some months, or even in one case two years, after they had finished the course, that they only now understood it.

Comments have also been made on various useful by-products of the course, such as that it has helped students to express themselves clearly, or to understand what people are trying to say, or to speak in public or to listen (the last a much-neglected skill).

On Suffering Change

IF a chimpanzee sees a mutilated head or an anaesthetized baby it shows fear (Hebb, 1946). When something is seen which is like a familiar object in some respects but not in all, that is, when there has been change, an animal may react as though it is frightened, whereas a completely strange thing may apparently have no effect. In this chapter I want to give evidence for my belief that much of the behaviour of the students in the discussion course can be understood in terms of their fear of change and their difficulties in adjusting to it, in bringing, that is, their old schemata into suitable relationships with new ones.

It is interesting to note how the importance of resistance to change is emphasized in two recent publications. In a note on the policy of the Josiah Macy, Jr. Foundation, of organizing group discussions on specialized aspects of scientific and medical research, the Director writes:

'The further conclusion has been reached as a result of this experiment, that the major obstructions to understanding among scientists lie in the resistance of human attitudes to change, rather than in difficulties of technical comprehension' (Fremont-Smith, 1956). Kennedy (1957), writing on a quite different subject, namely breakdown among senior management staff in industry, says that a great number of the breakdowns are directly related to a failure to adapt successfully to change, or the need for change.

The course presented to students a changed view of the external world and of their relations to it. Previously they had implicitly accepted the nineteenth-century view (Dingle, 1951); now they were seeing its limitations. The course challenged the student's assumption that he is a passive receiver of information from the outside world through his senses. The first three discussions showed how the knowledge of the external world obtained through sight is conditioned by one's own mental processes, and this shook the students' previously held belief in the concreteness and permanence of physical things. Examples of statements made after these revelations are 'It's as though my world has been cracked open'; 'But you can't have all the world a jelly'; 'I daren't walk downstairs in case the stairs aren't there'. At the same time the student was supported by seeing that everybody else's perceptions were equally subjective, and the discovery that even experts are affected by observer error (p. 90) was a special comfort to many.

From the point of view of intellectual functioning, as distinct from mental comfort, the ways in which resistance to change may affect thinking are of great importance. An example was frequently provided in the discussion on classification, where it was made clear that any one thing can belong to various different classes according to convenience. As we saw, however, many people felt strongly that there is somewhere a system of classification which does not depend on human convenience, which exists outside ourselves and is perfect, permanent and unchanging. They seemed to be expressing a desire to retain the notion of something fixed and eternal which exists independently of the vagaries of human needs.

Even more frightening than seeing the world change around one, may be seeing change in oneself. 'I can't trust myself now, let alone anyone else,' one man said after the first discussion. Sometimes a student may express a strong dislike for the idea that he could change. For instance one wrote, 'What have I gained from these discussions? Quite frankly I think nothing although subconsciously there may be a change. I may be more receptive to new ideas and I may be able to argue more concisely. . . . I would be sorry if I had changed to any great degree in so short a time. It would show, I think, unstability of former reasoning and I don't think that anyone would like to admit having such a radical fault as that.' In the same vein, some student might jeer at another who demonstrably changed his opinions during discussion, as though this was to be reprehended rather than approved. Here we see the great difficulty facing the teacher. Everything we are trying to teach can be learnt only if it is compatible with the student's present attitude, or if his attitude can be so modified as to incorporate it.

The impact of the course on the student is to be understood in relation to the more general changes to which he was subjected. Let us now look at some of these.

The student situation

Most of the students were between eighteen and twenty years old and had come to the University straight from school, having passed examinations in chemistry, physics and biology, exempting them from the First Medical Examination. They have the usual problems of changing from a condition of dependency to one of adult responsibility. For university students this change has special difficulties. They remain financially dependent, and the training period is prolonged into the age at which other people are earning their own living, getting married and having children.

To such well-recognized stresses that the change from school to university superimposes on the common stresses of growing up, the medical course adds others peculiar to itself. For a zoologist or a classicist the change in kind of study is not so marked—and he will have been taught at school by people who went through roughly the same university course. This is not so for a medical student, whose school-teachers will not have studied medicine, and whose classes in biology, physics and chemistry give him little preparation for dissecting the cadaver or experimenting on animals. And only a few years ahead he will be coping with matters not of greater responsibility perhaps, than those that await the engineer or atomic physicist, but of greater personal emotional involvement, concerning problems of suffering and disease, of birth, life and death. There were signs in the discussions that these matters already cast their shadows before them and gave rise to much heart searching—would it not be surprising (and indeed regrettable) otherwise? The talk for instance often turned to the doctor-patient relationship, the 'old-fashioned family doctor', the National Health Service, crowded surgeries, patients who have nothing the matter with them, the clinical training of medical students, relations with consultants and hospitals. It seemed that this was a way of helping to resolve the pressing doubts at the back of the minds—shall I be able to do this job?

I am not suggesting therefore that the preoccupation with the subject of change that I saw in the discussions was concerned only with the course itself, but rather that the intellectual matter of the course served to focus attention on problems concerned with change, and that the emotional climate permitted their ventilation.

Faced with the necessity to change, the problem arises to what extent is change in behaviour possible, to what extent are abilities fixed at birth, or at any rate by the time the students have come to the university? Discussion about the supposed stability of intelligence quotients, such questions as whether geniuses are born or made, the adequacy of various teaching and training techniques, methods of selection for universities and grammar schools, seemed to be ways of handling the essential problem—can I learn this new way of behaving?

Authority and dependence

The central problem seems to be the mass of difficulties associated with changing from a state of dependence on authority to that of full acceptance of adult responsibility. This is exemplified in the difference in relationship of pupil and teacher at university as compared with school. As we have seen, an exaggerated form of this new relationship is an essential feature of free group discussion, and required careful handling. At school the pressure of the examination system has been such that students tend to regard a teacher as one who supplied 'facts', and a teacher who does not do this may be resented. Some students were quite bewildered and said they were not learning anything at all, and thought that I must be conducting the course for my own good, since patently I was not doing it for theirs; that I was researching and not teaching, for they could not entertain the idea that it might be possible to do both at the same time. When hostility was openly expressed, as it often was in all sorts of ways, it was fairly easily countered. I explained that it takes some time to get used to new ideas and asked them to be patient and give the course a trial but to stay away if they still thought it was useless after the third or fourth discussion. It may be that statements designed to reassure the students that my intentions, at least, were not evil, may have helped to keep up the attendance, but they did not win the battle for understanding; they only made it not impossible to continue the fight. Whether openly expressed or not, hostility often took subtle forms and gave rise to curious confusions of thinking. To understand this it was necessary to learn to listen to a kind of 'double talk'. I shall give an example of this (and of the way in which I tried to deal with it) which illustrates how muddled thinking could not be cleared by rational argument because it reflected a strongly emotional reaction to a more general situation.

Double talk

Before the discussion started the students had written notes for twenty minutes on *Classification*. I asked *Mr. H* to open discussion, and he read with gusto from his script as follows:

'Classification—to put into classes, to segregate, the means whereby all things are organized for the benefit of learning and facilitation of reference. Classification exists primarily for the intelligentsia. For the ordinary citizen classification extends to a dictionary and financial organization, that is, the use of small metallic discs for bartering. (Appreciative laughter from members of the group.) Classification brings order into beautiful chaos, the state where actions and statements are not compared and unduly criticized. Classification is the major enemy of all individualistic tendencies but we, unfortunately, live in a civilization where individuals are sacrificed for the common good.'

It was already clear that *Mr. H* was discharging stronger feelings of distaste than most of us have about classification and it was possible that these feelings came, through association of schemata, from another source that had some of the characteristics, but not all, of classification. Might the statement 'Classification brings order into beautiful chaos, the state where actions and statements are not compared and unduly criticized' refer to the division of the class into groups for discussion? Might he (perhaps an 'ordinary citizen', not a member of the 'intelligentsia') be feeling that his individuality was being 'sacrificed for the common good'? For some time discussion was at cross purposes, the other students talking about commonly accepted meanings and implications of classification, *Mr. H* pursuing his more personal associations.

Mr. H was questioned a little about his remarks, and another student, *Miss G*, read parts of her script, saying that classification was a convenient system which simplified learning, a sort of catalogue and a sort of shorthand. She did not agree with *Mr. H* that it did any harm to the individual, though she said she saw what he meant. *Mr. H* elaborated his point thus:

'Things can be over classified by too much automation and telling you what to do. You must say this and you must do this and it's classified and set down in code and . . . well you're limited in your actions.' And later: 'Classification, order, all sorts of codes and civilizations. They all mean the same thing.'

Mr. C took him up: 'I think it's something which man has adopted so that he can understand more easily all the things that he finds in front of him which are infinitely varied,' and he gave examples.

Mr. H, however, was still involved with order and classification: 'I'm not against classification. I may have given you that idea, but I'm not, but I'm against over classification. Too much order . . . classification means putting into order.'

Mr. D: 'No, it means separating into groups.'

Mr. H: 'Of course, putting them into order is the same thing.'

And *Mr. E*, hitherto silent, came in: 'It's a different kind of order though, isn't it?'

I said that perhaps *Mr. H* was using 'order' in the sense of 'compel' or 'give orders', but he denied this, and four students tried to explain the confusion. I referred to the previous discussion on normal and recalled how overlapping meanings had confused thinking. *Mr. H* would have none of this:

'Well the only difficulty there is in communication, because you know what you're thinking, you know what you're meaning but other people don't understand you. That's the difficulty, the essential difficulty is communication. Not the confusion in your mind.'

(It seemed that he was referring to me and the discussions here: as though to say, you know what the discussions are about but you can't tell us.) *Mr. C* tried again to explain the effect of overlapping meanings, giving examples, but *Mr. H* could not follow him, and later he would not accept the suggestion that thinking is a kind of communicating with oneself:

> 'But then again it's still within the person, the person that's thinking knows what he's thinking usually.'

Some minutes later he agreed, as he had not previously done, that two meanings of 'order' were being used. I had said:

> 'I'm suggesting there is an association in your mind between the words "classification" and "order"; "order" meaning a tidy arrangement, orderliness, and "order" meaning a regulation or rule to which you have to conform.'

To which *Mr. H* replied: 'But you must say they're very close. In fact you can't really separate the two, can you?'

He continued to argue that to use a word in its double meanings did not confuse thinking. 'They most probably confuse your reception of my ideas, put it that way. They don't confuse me but they confuse you. . . . I mean you're the person who is confused with my ideas, not myself. . . . No, the only confusion lies in the fact that I have explained what I meant by classification and order and you don't agree; that's the confusion.'

And still later the following passage took place, in which *Mr. H* related the difficulty more directly to the work of the group:

> 'May I suggest that if this was not a discussion group there'd be no confusion in the use of any word at all. You'd accept them.'

Mr. F: 'There would probably still be confusion but you wouldn't talk about it.'

Mr. H: 'I don't think there would be as much confusion (laughter from the group), no—honestly.'

Mr. C: 'No, no you wouldn't be aware of it.'
Mr. F: 'It would still be there though, wouldn't it?'
Mr. H: 'I don't think so.'

After there had been some further argument about people misunderstanding each other which *Mr. H* said was due to not paying attention, or not hearing properly (rather than to semantic difficulties), I asked whether perhaps he was feeling that the difficulties about language were being invented in the discussion group? He said they were being pointed out, whereas in ordinary conversation they were passed over as unimportant. In reply to my question, did he think that was a good thing or a bad thing, he replied: 'I don't know quite honestly.'

I said perhaps he was feeling that we wasted time in these discussions?

Mr. H: 'No, the trouble is, you see, the difficulty is that we're quite used to having something given to us concrete with a sort of end point. Whereas these discussions you come in, you don't seem to be establishing anything. Maybe you are, I don't know, it's no sort of direct push to something, and if you're used to going towards something it's rather upsetting to start with.'

I replied: 'Yes, I think the discussions are very upsetting for quite a lot of people. . . . Well, they are simply designed to show you how you get information, the way your mind works when you're trying to get information. So there isn't, as it were, any direct thing that I can give you. Do you see? You've got to do it yourselves really.'

Mr. H: 'You can't give us a direct idea because of the difficulty in communication. You probably know what you are trying to achieve. But you can't communicate to us.'

I explained further that the skill of getting valid information from a given situation could not be learnt from verbal descriptions given by a teacher—as riding a bicycle could not. After a silence *Mr. H* said: 'What are we here for?' and this seemed the question that had worried him all the time.

The content of this passage can be interpreted in many

different ways. It may seem simply that *Mr. H* was confused about the meaning of the word 'classification' and that what he needed was a lecture on the subject. I do not think that a lecture would have helped him much at this particular time, because he was emotionally involved as well as intellectually confused. He denied that he himself was confused, and put the blame for our inability to agree with him on difficulties of communication, and on us. He refused to be put right by the other students who were not confused about this particular point. He expressed also resentment about regimentation in general which he alleged was involved in classification.

I am suggesting that *Mr. H*'s schemata about the meanings of words and about classification in particular, were interacting with his schemata about the aims of the discussion course, the relations of teacher and pupil, and of authoritative figures and dependants. For this reason, having failed to get clarification on the semantic difficulties, I invited him to express his criticism of the course, and his frustration and anxiety because my behaviour was not what he expected of a teacher. This hypothesis about the origin of *Mr. H*'s confusion about classification was supported by the nature of his contribution to the final discussion, in which the whole course was evaluated. Unlike most members of his group, *Mr. H* had found 'classification' the most interesting discussion. 'It was the one that went deepest,' he said. This remark is to be assessed in relation to the fact that the rational content of *Mr. H*'s contribution to 'classification' cited here (and this is the major part of his contribution) cannot be regarded as showing much grasp of what others regarded as the main topic of discussion; it could not be called 'deep' in the intellectual sense. Nor can I find in *Mr. H*'s contribution to the later part of the discussion any indication that he had by then modified his schemata in such a way as to take in the abundance of information about classification which the rest of us had painstakingly laid before him. The problem of readjusting his ideas about the relation of himself to those in authority was for him at that time of greater urgency than the problem of the uses of classification, and through his double-talk he ventilated both together. I suggest that he felt that this discussion 'went deeper' because through it he became clearer, not so much on classification as on the aims of the course and his need to change his perception of his relations to authority to adapt to it.

A student, *Mr. X*, in another group met the challenge of the course in quite a different way. Already in the first meeting he appreciated the far-reaching implications of the discussion of hand radiographs:

> 'It's so long that we have taken for granted what we're told, that to turn round not only what we're told but everything. . . .'

He was sharply critical of the method of teaching as being too destructive. In the third discussion he accused me of asking the students to throw away the key they could use, before they were able to use another (he referred to writing music). Later he insisted:

> '. . . one still keeps the hard core—the majority of assumptions work in the majority of situations. . . . The hard core of our living, our day-to-day living, is secure, and I stick to the word very firmly, and that we do question, we question a lot, but on the periphery, where our knowledge is expanding into new ground. And we're so taken up with this expansion into new ground, and get so worried that some of these assumptions are being questioned, that we tend to work backwards and question the whole of the hard core. And in fact it's very, very stupid to do so. . . .'

The replies of two other students are given to illustrate the point I made on page 80, that often the teacher can soon abdicate, and the sooner the better.

Mr. Y: 'All you know is that the assumptions were secure as far as you know, and are now as far as you know, whether they will be or not. . . . Whether some of these basic assumptions will suddenly be altered tomorrow you don't know. To call them a hard core gives them a sense of permanence which they shouldn't have if you're going to be able to question these . . . fringes as you say.'

Mr. Z: 'These are certain assumptions which work in a greater number of cases than other assumptions and therefore you can call them a harder core than the rest, but you can't say that every, any particular assumption works in absolutely every instance, because surely that is what we saw with the revolving window frame. (He refers to one of the illusions demonstrated.) We thought that was an assumption which always worked, well it obviously doesn't. And we may, might have thought it to have been one of the assumptions that make up a hard core, and realize that even a basic assumption like that is destroyable.'

Mr. Y: 'If I can bring in an analogy you seem to be as if when learning to skate, trying to find a nice hard piece of ice which you can stand upright on instead of trying to learn how to move on it. You continue trying to find something, some foundation piece which will not move, whereas everything will move and you've got to learn to skate on it.'

In the fifth discussion *Mr. X* talked of people having their experience in boxes, and these boxes must be broken to let new experience in; he seemed to complain that I was not permitting them to do this, behaviour which is scarcely compatible with what he had complained of before. In the final discussion *Mr. X* said:

'. . . I think the thing about it is that our basic assumptions are as important in medical subjects as the actual knowledge . . . therefore to a medical student, as important as acquiring knowledge of anatomy, is the examination of our basic assumptions and the realization that these must be made to grow and develop along with your knowledge.'

Mr. X, unlike *Mr. H*, expressed his fears and criticisms openly from the beginning, and throughout commented freely on his own changing perceptions of the course, using different symbols with his changing mood. *Mr. X*'s schemata concerning the relation of teacher and pupil, and his own relation to the external world in general, had been activated by the discussion, as had *Mr. H*'s, but in *Mr. X*'s case they were separable from the schemata concerning the subject matter of the course, while in *Mr. H*'s case they were confused with them.

The need for continual change

To summarize, the course demonstrated to the student his own personal involvement with his perception of the external world. It showed to what an extraordinary extent the information he received from any situation depended on his own assumptions or preconceptions. Consequently his belief in the stability and independence of the external world and his confidence in his ability to secure reliable information about it were shaken. Not only is 'authority' to be questioned (a recommendation which is fortunately often attractive to the young) but himself—the validity of his own judgments. The course brought the student face to face with the need for continual change in himself, if he is to take in more of the information available to him. In some circumstances, such a message could be so painful that it would be rejected. I regard a lot of my work in the discussions as directed towards making it acceptable. The aim was to make it possible for the student to relinquish the security of thinking in well-defined, given channels and to find a new kind of stability based on the recognition and acceptance of ambiguity, uncertainty and open choice.

Argument

THE argument of this book runs as follows. In receiving information from a given stimulus pattern we select from the total amount of information available (that is, from the complex of the stimulus pattern in its context) and from our own store of information. The receipt of information therefore involves making a judgment, but in many cases (as for instance in seeing familiar things) this is done so rapidly and automatically that we are unaware of the extent of our personal involvement in the act, tending to regard the information as given. In such cases we might obtain more valid information if we could consider alternative selections from the information available.

Many factors of which we are unconscious influence our judgments, both in cases where we are not aware of making any (as in seeing) and in those where we are (as in evaluating evidence from an experiment). It is postulated that we might make more valid judgments if we could become conscious of some of these factors. A situation (free group discussion) is described in which alternative judgments of the same stimulus pattern are discussed, and some of the factors influencing the judgments become apparent. The validity of the contribution of the various factors can then be assessed. The results of a test support the hypothesis that judgment is improved after this experience.

Appendix

Bibliography

Index

Fig. 12. The Hidden Man revealed

Bibliography

ABERCROMBIE, M. L. JOHNSON, see JOHNSON, M. L.

AMES, A. 1955. *An interpretive manual for the demonstrations in the psychology research centre*, Princeton University. Princeton: Princeton University Press.

BARTLETT, F. C. 1932. *Remembering*. Cambridge: Cambridge University Press.

BAUER, M. A. and JOHNSON, M. L. 1946. *The Scientific value of Higher School Certificate Zoology*. School Science Review, **103**, 384.

BEXTON, W. H., HERON, W. and SCOTT, T. H. 1954. *Effects of decreased variation in the sensory environment*. Canad. J. Psychol. **8**, 70.

BINDRA, D. 1956. In *Discussions on child development*. Vol. 2, edited by J. M. Tanner and B. Inhelder. London: Tavistock Publications.

BION, W. R. 1948–51. *Experiences in groups*. Human Relations, **1**, 314, 487; **2**, 13, 195; **3**, 3, 395; **4**, 221.

BIRKELO, C. C., CHAMBERLAIN, W. E., PHELPS, P. S., SCHOOLS, P. E., ZACKS, D. and YERUSHALMY, J. 1957. *Tuberculosis case finding*. J. Amer. Med. Assoc. **133**, 359.

BLAKE, R. V. and RAMSEY, G. V. 1951. *Perception—an approach to personality*. New York: The Ronald Press Company.

Blakiston's New Gould medical dictionary. 1949. London: Lewis.

BOWLBY, J. 1951. *Maternal care and mental health*. Geneva: W. H. O. Monograph Series.

BRESSLER, B. J. 1931. *Illusion in the case of subliminal perception*. J. Gen. Psychol., **5**, 244.

BREUIL, H. 1952. *Four hundred centuries of cave art*. Montignac: Windels.

BROWN, G. BALDWIN. 1928. *The art of the cave dweller*. London: Murray.

BRUNER, J. S. 1951. *Personality dynamics and the process of perceiving*, in Blake and Ramsey, q.v.

BRUNER, J. S., GOODNOW, JACQUELINE, J. and AUSTIN, GEORGE A. 1956. *A study of thinking.* London: Chapman and Hall.

BRUNER, J. S. and POSTMAN, L. 1949. *On the perception of incongruity: a paradigm.* J. Person., **18**, 206.

BURT, C. 1947. *Transfer of Training.* Universities Quarterly, **1**, 281.

CARMICHAEL, L., HOGAN, H. P. and WALTERS, A. A. 1932. *An experimental study of the effect of language on the reproduction of visually perceived form.* J. Exper. Psychol., **15**, 73.

CARTWRIGHT, D. and ZANDER, A. 1953 (Eds.). *Group dynamics: research and theory.* London: Tavistock.

CRAWSHAY-WILLIAMS, R. 1947. *The comforts of unreason.* London: Routledge and Kegan Paul.

CROFTON, J. W., FAWCETT, J. W., JAMES, D. G., SCADDING, J. C., MACRAE, A. D. and MARMION, B. P. 1951. *Pneumonia in West London*, 1949–50. Brit. Med. J., *ii*, 1368.

DARWIN, C. 1859. *The Origin of Species.* London: Murray.

DAVIS, D. R. and SINHA, D. 1950. *The influence of an interpolated experience upon recognition.* Q. J. Exp. Psychol., **2**, 43.

DINGLE, H. 1951. *A Century of Science.* London: Hutchinson.

DORLAND, W. A. 1947. *The American illustrated medical dictionary.* London: Saunders.

DUNLAP, K. 1900. *The effect of imperceptible shadows on the judgement of distance.* Psychol. Rev., **7**, 435.

Faber Medical Dictionary. 1953. London: Faber and Faber.

FOULKES, S. H. and ANTHONY, J. A. 1957. *Group psychotherapy.* Harmondsworth: Penguin Books.

FREMONT-SMITH, F. 1956. In Schaffner, 1956, q.v.

GESELL, A., ILG, F. L. and BULLIS, G. 1949. *Vision, its development in the child.* New York: Harper.

GIBSON, E. J. 1953. *A survey of research on improvement in perceptual judgements as a function of controlled practice and training.* Research Bulletin, 53–45. Texas: Human Resources Research Center.

GOLDFARB, W. 1943. *The effects of early institutional care on adolescent personality.* J. Exp. Educ., **12**, 106.

GREGG, A. 1949. *The Golden Gate of Medicine.* Annals Intern. Med., **30**, 810.

HARE, A. P., BORGATTA, E. F. and BALES, R. F. 1955. *Small groups: studies in social interaction.* New York: Knopf.

HEATH, C. W. *et al.* 1945. *What people are: a study of normal young men.* Cambridge, Mass.: Harvard University Press.

HEBB, D. O. 1946. *On the nature of fear.* Psychol. Rev., **53**, 257.

—— 1949. *Organization of behaviour.* London: Chapman and Hall.

—— 1955. *Drives and the conceptual nervous system.* Psychol. Rev., **62**, 243.

ITTELSON, W. H. and CANTRIL, H. 1954. *Perception, a transactional approach.* New York: Doubleday.

JAMES, D. W., JOHNSON, M. L. and VENNING, P. 1956. *Testing for learnt skill in observation and evaluation of evidence.* Lancet, *ii*, 379.

JOHNSON, M. L. 1948. *Biology and training in scientific method.* School Science Review, **108**, 139.

—— 1950. *Discussion methods in preclinical teaching.* Lancet, *ii*, 313.

—— 1955. *Observer error; its bearing on teaching.* Lancet, *ii*, 422.

JONES, E. 1942. *The concept of the normal mind.* Internat. J. Psycho-Analysis, **23**, 1.

KELLER, H. 1914. *The story of my life.* 8th ed. London: Hodder and Stoughton.

KENNEDY, A. 1957. *Individual reactions to change as seen in senior management in industry.* Lancet, *i*, 261.

KILPATRICK, F. P. 1952. *Human behaviour from the transactional point of view.* Hanover N. H.: Hanover Inst. for Assoc. Res.

KING, C. DALY. 1945. *The meaning of normal.* Yale J. Biol. and Med., **17**, 493.

KLAPMAN, J. W. 1946. *Group psychotherapy: Theory and practice.* London: Heinemann.

KLEIN, J. 1956. *The study of groups.* London: Routledge and Kegan Paul.

Lancet. 1954. *Observer error, i*, 87.

—— 1955. *By any other name, i*, 1257.

LEASON, P. A. 1939. *A new view of the Western European group of Quarternary art.* Proc. Prehist. Soc. N.S., **5**, 51.

——1956. *Obvious facts of Quaternary cave art.* Medical and Biological Illustration, **6**, 209.

LEWES, G. H. 1879. *Problems of life and mind.* London: Trübner.

LEWIN, K. 1953. *Studies in group decision,* in Cartwright and Zander. 1953, q.v.

LUQUET, G. H. 1923. *Le réalisme dans l'art paléolithique.* L'Anthropologie, **33**, 17.

LYON, D. M. 1942. *What do we mean by 'Normal'?* Clinical Journal, **71**, 239.

MACK, J. A. 1956. Review of *Growing up in the City* by John Barren Mays. Brit. J. Psychol., **46**, 321.

McKELLAR, F. 1957. *Imagination and thinking.* London: Cohen and West.

METCALFE, M. 1956. Review of *La Notion de normal en Psychologie clinique* by FR. DUYCKAERTS. Brit. J. Psychol., **46**, 319.

MILLER, J. G. 1951. *Unconscious processes and perception,* in Blake and Ramsey, 1951, q.v.

MORENO, J. L. 1945 (Ed.) *Group psychotherapy, a symposium.* New York: Beacon House.

OLDFIELD, R. C. and ZANGWILL, O. L. 1942–3. *Head's concept of the schema and its application in contemporary British psychology.* Brit. J. Psychol., **32**, 267; **33**, 58, 113, 143.

PIAGET, J. 1929. *The child's conception of the world.* London: Kegan Paul, Trench, Trübner and Co. Ltd.

—— 1932. *The moral judgement of the child.* London. Kegan Paul, Trench, Trübner and Co. Ltd.

—— 1955. *The child's construction of reality.* London: Routledge and Kegan Paul Ltd.

PRICE, H. W. 1932. *Perception.* London: Methuen.

RENBOURN, E. T. and Ellison, J. McK. 1950. *Some errors in gas analysis using the Haldane apparatus.* J. Hyg., **48**, 239.

Report on Medical Education from the Planning Committee. Royal College of Physicians. 1944.

REVESZ, G. 1950. *Psychology and art of the blind.* London: Longmans Green.

RIESEN, A. H. 1947. *The development of visual perception in man and chimpanzees.* Science, **106**, 107.

ROSEBOROUGH, M. E. 1953. *Experimental studies of small groups.* Psychol. Bull., **50**, 275.

RUESCH, J. and BATESON, G. 1951. *Communication, the social matrix of society.* New York: W. W. Norton.

RYLE, J. A. 1947. *The meaning of normal.* Lancet, *i*, 1.

SCHAFFNER, B. (Editor). 1956. *Group Processes, transactions of 2nd Conference.* New York: Josiah Macy Jr. Foundation.

SENDEN, M. 1932. Quoted Hebb, 1949, q.v.

Shorter Oxford English Dictionary. 1952. Oxford: Clarendon Press.

SLADEN, W. J. L. 1956. In Schaffner, 1956, q.v.

SLAVSON, S. R. 1950. *Analytic group psychotherapy with children, adolescents and adults.* New York: Columbia University Press.

Stedman's Medical Dictionary. 1954. London; Baillière, Tindall and Cox.

STRODTBECK, F. L. and HARE, A. P. 1954. *Bibliography of small group research (from 1900 through 1953).* Sociometry, **17,** 107.

TAYLOR, F. SHERWOOD. 1932. *Inorganic and theoretical chemistry.* London: Heinemann.

TROTTER, W. F. 1916. *Instincts of the Herd in Peace and War.* London: Fisher Unwin.

VERNON, M. D. 1952. *A further study of perception.* Cambridge: Cambridge University Press.

—— 1955. *The functions of schemata in perceiving.* Psychol. Rev., **62,** 180.

WARREN, H. C. 1934. *Dictionary of Psychology.* Boston: Houghton Mifflin.

Webster's New International Dictionary. 1934. London: Bell.

WHITE, R. and LIPPITT, R. 1953. *Leader behaviour and member reaction in three 'social climates'.* In Cartwright and Zander, 1953, q.v.

WOLTERS, A. W. 1943. *Some biological aspects of thinking.* Brit. J. Psychol., **33,** 176.

YERUSHALMY, J., GARLAND, L. H., HARKNESS, J. T., HINSHAW, H. C., MILLER, E. R., SHIPMAN, S. J. and ZWERLING, H. B. 1951. *An evaluation of the role of serial chest roentgenograms in estimating the progress of disease in patients with pulmonary tuberculosis.* Amer. Rev. Tuberculosis, **64,** 225.

YOUNG, J. Z. 1951. *Doubt and Certainty in Science.* Oxford: Clarendon Press.

Index

Index

153

UNIVERSITY LIBRARY
LOMA LINDA, CALIFORNIA

UNIVERSITY LIBRARY
LOMA LINDA, CALIFORNIA